AF446903

LGBTQ+ GUIDE TO MIXED-ORIENTATION MARRIAGES

Strategies for Emotional Resilience, Identity Exploration and Coming Out, Real-Life Success Stories, and Legal and Financial Advice

---

ALEX HARPER

Copyright Alex Harper 2024 - All rights reserved.

The content within this book may not be reproduced, duplicated or transmitted without direct written permission from the author or the publisher.

Under no circumstances will any blame or legal responsibility be held against the publisher or author for any damages, reparation, or monetary loss due to the information contained within this book. Either directly or indirectly. You are responsible for your own choices, actions, and results.

<u>Legal Notice:</u>

This book is copyright-protected and only for personal use. You cannot amend, distribute, sell, use, quote, or paraphrase any part of the content without the consent of the author or publisher.

<u>Disclaimer Notice:</u>

Please note that the information in this document is for educational and entertainment purposes only. All effort has been expended to present accurate, up-to-date, reliable, and complete information. No warranties of any kind are declared or implied. Readers acknowledge that the author does not render legal, financial, medical, or professional advice. The content within this book has been derived from various sources. Please consult a licensed professional before attempting any techniques outlined in this book.

By reading this document, the reader agrees that the author is under no circumstances responsible for any direct or indirect losses incurred from using the information contained within this document, including, but not limited to, errors, omissions, or inaccuracies.

Contents

Introduction

A recent survey found that a significant number of mixed-orientation marriages exist quietly at the intersection of love and complexity within the LGBTQ+ community. These relationships, where one partner is heterosexual and the other identifies as LGBTQ+, unfold stories of love, challenge, and profound discovery. This book seeks to explore and understand these stories with their rich emotional backgrounds.

Mixed-orientation marriages are as diverse as the individuals who make them up, and each story carries its unique blend of challenges and triumphs. With sensitivity and an inclusive lens, this book delves into the nuanced experiences of these couples, acknowledging the vast spectrum of identities and experiences within the LGBTQ+ community.

This book's purpose is twofold: to offer a supportive, insightful guide for those navigating their journey in a mixed-orientation marriage and to enrich the broader dialogue about these relationships. Through a blend of personal stories, expert psychological insights, and practical legal and financial advice, this work is a comprehensive resource for understanding and thriving in these relationships

In the following chapters, we will explore various aspects of mixed-orientation marriages—from the initial stages of understanding and acceptance to the complexities of maintaining intimacy and navigating societal pressures. Each chapter is designed to build upon the last, creating a cohesive guide that will equip you with the knowledge and tools to foster a thriving relationship.

To you, the reader, whether you are in a mixed-reading orientation marriage yourself or seeking to support someone who is, this book is for you. It acknowledges your challenges and offers strategies for resilience and understanding. It's a space where your experiences are seen and valued.

Let me share a quote that touched me deeply and which I believe captures the essence of our journey through this book: "Love is not something we give or get; it is something that we nurture and grow." This statement is a reminder of the dynamic, evolving nature of relationships and the continuous effort they require.

As we progress, I invite you to engage deeply with this material. Reflect on your own experiences, jot down thoughts, and find echoes of your life in the shared stories. This book is not just to be read; it's to be experienced.

Let us begin this journey with an open heart and mind, ready to understand more deeply, support more strongly, and love more fully. Here's to finding joy, understanding, and fulfillment in the beautiful complexity of your unique relationship.

ONE

Understanding Mixed-Orientation Marriages

Did you know that the term 'mixed-orientation marriage' isn't just a fancy way to stir up drama in soap operas? Oh no, it's a real-life dynamic where one spouse might be planning a surprise party, and the other might just be planning their coming-out party. Jokes aside, these marriages are a profound intersection of love, identity, and, sometimes, a sprinkle of confusion, embodying a spectrum of identities and orientations. In this chapter, let's unwrap this layered concept together, peeling back the definitions, dynamics, and impacts with the care of someone trying to sneak a midnight snack without waking anyone up.

Defining Mixed-Orientation Marriage: More Than Just Labels

So, what do we mean by mixed-orientation marriages? It's not just about who likes whom. It's about recognizing the full range of human sexuality within a marriage. One partner might be straight, while the other could be lesbian, gay, bisexual, transgender, LGBTQ+, questioning, intersex or asexual (LGBTQ+). It's not about fitting people into categories but understanding that these identities are diverse and varied.

Think about it; the relationships under this umbrella are incredibly diverse. Some couples start their marriage with open acknowledgment of their orientations. Picture a scene where both partners are upfront about their identities from their first coffee date, navigating their marriage with this knowledge at the forefront. On the flip side, there are marriages where one partner might come to realize and disclose their orientation years down the line, turning what was a presumed traditional marriage into a mixed-orientation relationship. This could happen during a typical Tuesday dinner or a joint Netflix binge-watch session.

Why is it crucial for us to get these terms right and truly understand them? Because, my dear reader, understanding fosters empathy and support, not just within the marriage but from society as well. When we recognize and validate these relationships, we're not just being nice; we're being human. We're acknowledging that love, in its essence, is diverse and that it can thrive under various circumstances.

Let's talk about the impact of these differing orientations on the dynamics within a marriage. Well, they can stir up everything from emotional intimacy to long-term expectations. For instance, sexual relationships might require renegotiation or redefinition, which isn't a walk in the park or a walk anywhere really—it's more of a deep, meaningful dance, sometimes stepping on each other's toes until you find the rhythm that works for both. Emotional intimacy, too, might need a tune-up. It's about finding new ways to connect that resonate with both partners, ensuring everyone feels valued and understood.

One must consider the rollercoaster of emotions and logistical puzzles that might arise in exploring these dynamics. However, it's also about recognizing the potential for growth and deeper bonding that such challenges can introduce. Who said puzzles were only meant for rainy days? In mixed-orientation marriages, solving puzzles daily provides opportunities to understand and love each other more deeply.

Interactive Element: Reflection Section

Take a moment to jot down some thoughts:

- How do you currently define your relationship dynamics?
- What aspects of your partnership could benefit from a deeper understanding of each other's orientations?

As we continue to explore these themes, remember this isn't just about navigating challenges; it's about celebrating the diversity of love. So, let's keep turning the pages, shall we? Your snack awaits in the next section, and trust me, it's worth staying up for.

The Spectrum of Sexuality in Marriage: Beyond Gay and Straight

Think of sexuality not just as a line from gay to straight but more like a sprawling vineyard with a wide variety of grapes, each with its unique flavor profile. In the context of mixed-orientation marriages, understanding this spectrum—encompassing bisexual, pansexual, asexual, and many other identities—is like understanding that wine isn't just red or white. There's a whole range in between, each adding a distinct taste to the blend that is a marriage.

For instance, let's consider a marriage where one partner identifies as bisexual. This orientation doesn't always mean an equal attraction to all genders, as some might oversimplify it. Instead, it could manifest as changing attractions and preferences over time, introducing flexibility and complexity into the marital dynamics. Imagine this scenario: a bisexual spouse might feel their attractions fluctuate, which could lead to discussions about boundaries, monogamy, or openness in the marriage that might not be as prevalent in other marriages. This fluidity doesn't dilute the commitment; it just adds different ingredients to the marriage pot, needing stirring and sometimes a little spice to get it just right.

Then, consider a partner who is asexual, where sexual attraction might not be the driving force of their relationship. Here, emotional intimacy becomes the cornerstone. Think of it like a dance where the steps are less about passion and more about synchronizing perfectly with the music of mutual respect and deep connection. These couples might find intimacy in shared interests, deep conversations, or simply the comfort of being in each other's presence, crafting a relationship deeply rooted in companionship.

However, navigating these diverse orientations isn't without its hurdles. A common challenge is the lack of understanding or misconceptions from the outside world and the relationship itself. For instance, asexual individuals often face misconceptions that they are just 'uninterested in sex' rather than understanding it as a genuine identity, leading to unnecessary pressures or feelings of inadequacy. Bisexual individuals might confront doubts about their fidelity or commitment, stemming from stereotypes that label them as indecisive or greedy. It's like trying to fit a complex jigsaw puzzle when others only hand you pieces from another set: frustrating and unhelpful.

Educational insights from recent psychological and sociological research tell us that acknowledging and understanding these diverse sexual orientations can significantly enrich a relationship. Studies suggest that when partners in a mixed-orientation marriage openly discuss and genuinely recognize each other's sexual identities, it can lead to higher levels of satisfaction and deeper intimacy. It's like a map in a treasure hunt; knowing the lay of the land doesn't make the treasure less valuable—it makes the path to finding it more navigable and the journey more enjoyable.

Incorporating this understanding into marriage goes beyond just knowing the terms. It means including them in daily interactions, conversations, and decisions. It's about creating a space where each partner feels truly seen and valued for who they are, including their sexual orientation. This approach improves personal interactions and sets a strong example of inclusivity and acceptance in a world that often tries to simplify human identity.

Common Misunderstandings About Mixed-Orientation Marriages

Let's talk turkey about some of the myths swirling around mixed-orientation marriages. You know, those prepackaged notions that get passed around like last year's holiday fruitcake. First up, the big one: the inevitability of divorce. It seems like society expects these marriages to have the shelf life of a ripe banana. But let's peel back that myth. While it's true that mixed-orientation marriages can face unique challenges, the divorce rate isn't automatically higher than in any other marriage. It's not about the orientation but how the individuals handle relationship dynamics, communication, and mutual respect. Just because a marriage dances to a different beat doesn't mean it can't last the whole party.

Another hot take that needs cooling off is that love alone can bulldoze through any issue, including fundamental differences in orientation. While love is a powerful and necessary ingredient in any marriage, it's not the cure-all. Think of it like trying to fix a leaky roof with a lovely bouquet of roses—beautiful, but not particularly helpful. Couples in mixed-orientation marriages also need tools like open communication, boundary-setting, and, sometimes, counseling to navigate their unique complexities. Love gets you into the dance, but the steps you take together keep you from stepping on each other's toes.

Then there's the persistent myth that all mixed-orientation marriages are just ticking time bombs of unhappiness. Let's bust that myth with a dose of reality. Many couples in such marriages experience deep satisfaction and joy in their relationships. These marriages can be just as fulfilling, loving, and vibrant as any other—sometimes even more so because of the heightened communication and understanding required. Every marriage has hills and valleys; the scenery might look slightly different.

Let's sprinkle in some facts and figures to solidify our myth-busting. Studies have shown that relationship satisfaction in mixed-orientation marriages can be high, provided the relationship is built on honesty, mutual respect, and realistic expectations. For instance, a study by the Journal of Marriage and Family found that when both partners are committed to the relationship and open about their needs, these marriages can thrive just like their all-heterosexual or all-homosexual counterparts.

Changing societal norms and stereotypes is crucial in how these relationships are perceived and experienced. The more society understands and accepts the fluidity of human sexuality, the easier it is for individuals in mixed-orientation marriages to feel supported rather than stigmatized. It's like moving from a black-and-white TV to full-color HD—suddenly, there's a lot more nuance and clarity, which enriches everyone's viewing experience.

Let's illustrate with real-life examples, minus the names, to keep things confidential. Consider the case of a couple where one partner came out as gay several years into their marriage. Initially, shock and uncertainty clouded their future. However, with counseling and a strong commitment to their family, they navigated these uncharted waters and reshaped their marriage into a partnership based on deep friendship and co-parenting. Their story shows that mixed-orientation marriages can adapt and flourish with the right support and dedication.

Or take another couple who entered their marriage knowing full well about their different orientations. They've built a robust marriage that defies the stereotypes by setting clear expectations and boundaries, engaging in ongoing dialogue about their needs, and fostering a strong emotional connection based on mutual interests and shared values. Their journey underscores the importance of transparency and honesty from the get-go.

These cases show that while mixed-orientation marriages might require different handling, the core ingredients for a successful marriage—respect, love, and communication—are universal. By debunking myths and understanding the real dynamics at play, we can help ensure that all marriages, regardless of orientation, are given the chance to succeed and thrive.

The History and Evolution of Mixed-Orientation Marriages

When we flip through the pages of history, mixed-orientation marriages aren't a chapter boldly highlighted; often, they're a footnote subtly tucked in the margins. Yet, their existence and the evolving perceptions around them paint a fascinating picture of societal change. Historically, many mixed-orientation marriages were products of societal pressures, where conforming to heterosexual norms was not just expected but practically enforced. Everyone was supposed to fit the same mold; if you didn't, you had to pretend you did.

Fast forward to the last few decades, and you'll see the narrative beginning to shift. The latter half of the 20th century marked a significant period as the LGBTQ+ rights movements began to gain momentum, challenging long-standing norms and advocating for the recognition and rights of LGBTQ+ individuals. This advocacy played a crucial role in shifting public perception, gradually transforming mixed-orientation marriages from a hidden reality to a recognized identity. Think of it as moving from whispered conversations behind closed doors to open discussions at the dinner table.

Legal and cultural milestones have significantly influenced how these marriages are viewed and treated. For instance, the decriminalization of homosexuality in many parts of the world was a turning point. It meant that being in a mixed-orientation marriage wasn't just a personal struggle but a legal one, too, fighting against a backdrop of laws that didn't recognize or protect the rights of LGBTQ+ individuals. Then came the landmark rulings on same-sex marriage, like the Obergefell v. Hodges case in 2015 in the United States, which didn't just make headlines; it rewrote them, providing legal recognition and a slew of rights previously denied to many couples in mixed-orientation marriages.

Looking across cultures, the acceptance and treatment of mixed-orientation marriages vary widely. In some places, progressive attitudes and laws have paved the way for greater acceptance and support. In others, traditional beliefs and the lack of legal protections continue to challenge these couples. It's a bit like a global patchwork quilt, each piece representing a different approach based on cultural, legal, and social fabrics. For example, increased visibility and support for LGBTQ+ rights in many Western societies have fostered a more accepting environment. Contrast this with several countries where LGBTQ+ rights are still heavily suppressed, and the challenges become starkly apparent.

The impact of LGBTQ+ movements in increasing the visibility and acceptance of mixed-orientation marriages cannot be overstated. These movements have not only championed the cause of equal rights but have also helped to educate the public, dismantle stereotypes, and promote a broader understanding of the beautiful diversity within human relationships. They've turned up the volume on conversations that were once only whispers, empowering people to live authentically in their relationships and encouraging society to accept them without prejudice.

Looking at the history of mixed-orientation marriages, we've made progress, but there's still a long way to go. Today's changes come from people who dared to love openly and activists who worked hard for every bit of progress in rights and recognition. This shows the power of resilience and the ongoing fight for equality, reminding us that every effort matters in the bigger picture of human history.

Psychological Impacts on Partners in Mixed-Orientation Marriages

Navigating a mixed-orientation marriage can often feel like trying to read a map in the dark. It's not just about finding your way. It's about recalibrating the journey occasionally to ensure both partners are on the same path. The emotional and psychological challenges faced by LGBTQ+ and heterosexual partners in these marriages are as varied as they are profound. Each partner may grapple with different emotional challenges, and understanding these nuances is critical to maintaining the relationship's health and each partner's well-being.

For the LGBTQ+ partner, the act of coming out—or, in some cases, coming to terms with their orientation within the marriage—can be a cathartic but daunting process. It's like finally deciding to climb the mountain you've always been afraid to approach. The relief of embracing one's true self is often shadowed by fear of rejection or causing hurt, leading to a complex mix of liberation and guilt. On the flip side, the heterosexual partner might experience a whirlwind of confusion and betrayal, mixed with the need to support the person they love. They might be struggling with what this revelation means for their identity and imagined future, now feeling uncertain and worried about what lies ahead.

Effective coping mechanisms are crucial in navigating these choppy waters. Therapy, without a doubt, plays a significant role. Engaging with a therapist who specializes in LGBTQ+ issues can provide a safe space to explore these feelings without judgment. Couples therapy is also beneficial, allowing both partners to share their fears, hopes, and frustrations. It's like having an experienced guide to help you through tough times. Besides professional help, developing personal coping strategies such as mindfulness, open communication, and setting time aside for individual and shared activities can help maintain emotional balance and reduce stress. These activities help keep you emotionally healthy and grounded.

The impact on identity for both partners can be significant. For the LGBTQ+ partner, integrating their sexual orientation with their identity might feel like rediscovering themselves in a new light. It's a process that can be refreshing and intimidating as they reassess what they want from life and their marriage. For the heterosexual partner, there might be a struggle with their self-image and feelings of insecurity about what their spouse's orientation means about them. "Am I enough?" becomes a recurring question in their mind, muddying their sense of self-worth. Both partners might need to redefine their roles within the marriage, which can be confusing but necessary. It's like realizing you must adjust to new circumstances partway through the journey.

Drawing upon insights from psychologists specializing in mixed-orientation marriages, it becomes clear that these relationships can indeed thrive, provided there is a continuous effort toward mutual understanding and growth. These professionals emphasize the importance of each partner maintaining their individuality while finding common ground to nurture their relationship. It's not about conforming to the other but about adapting to create a partnership that respects and celebrates their differences.

Navigating the psychological impacts of a mixed-orientation marriage is no small feat. It requires patience, love, and a willingness to adapt to each other's needs continually. Like any profound journey, it's fraught with challenges but also filled with opportunities for growth and deeper connection. As we explore these dynamics, remember that the goal isn't to eliminate the differences but to integrate them into a stronger, more resilient relationship.

The Role of Societal Perception in Mixed-Orientation Marriages

Let's consider this: How does society, with all its unwritten rules and glossy magazine ideals, really influence the details of a mixed-orientation marriage? Societal norms and expectations can either support a relationship or restrict its growth. For couples in mixed-orientation marriages, these societal standards often shape not just how they view themselves but also how stable and satisfied they feel in their relationships.

Imagine living in a neighborhood where every house is expected to look the same, but yours has a wild, beautiful garden that doesn't fit the mold. That's what it's like navigating a mixed-orientation marriage in a society with rigid expectations about relationships. These couples often face pressures to conform to traditional marriage paradigms—white picket fences, 2.5 kids, a dog, and matching bathrobes. Deviating from this can sometimes lead to feelings of instability within the marriage as partners grapple with external perceptions while managing their internal dynamics. It's not just about keeping the garden tidy; it's about ensuring it thrives despite the nosy neighbors.

Now, let's talk about the giant, flashy billboard that is media representation. How often do you see mixed-orientation marriages portrayed in films or on TV? And when they are, are they the heartwarming main story or just a dramatic subplot designed to tug at heartstrings before sweeping the complexity under the rug? More often than not, the media portrays these relationships under a distressing lens, emphasizing turmoil and tragedy over the everyday joys and challenges. This skewed representation can seep into public perception, influencing how society views these marriages and how those in them feel seen and valued—or not.

Community support, or the lack of it, can make or break these marriages. Access to resources and networks that understand and affirm the unique aspects of mixed-orientation marriages can make a difference. Whether counseling services, social groups, or even online forums, having a community that nods along and says, "We get it," can help couples navigate societal challenges more confidently. With robust community support, navigating societal expectations becomes less about surviving and more about thriving.

And here's where we roll up our sleeves—advocacy and change. Encouraging a more inclusive understanding and support system for mixed-orientation marriages is crucial. It's about painting new signs, telling new stories, and changing the narrative from misunderstanding to celebration. Advocacy can take many forms, from pushing for more accurate representations in media to supporting legislation that protects and recognizes the rights of all marriages, regardless of orientation. It's about looking out for everyone's well-being and respecting and valuing every relationship.

Considering all these factors—from societal norms to advocacy's concrete actions—it becomes clear that the world of mixed-orientation marriages is complex. But it's also full of opportunities for growth, change, and deeper understanding. It's about turning small talks into meaningful conversations, breaking down barriers, and creating relationships that thrive and stand out.

TWO

Coming Out in Marriage

Picture this: you're backstage, the curtains are about to draw, and you're about to step into the spotlight, not to belt out a show-tune, but to share a truth about yourself that might change everything. Coming out in a mixed-orientation marriage often feels like a high-stakes performance where the script has yet to be written. It's profoundly personal, occasionally messy, and requires a blend of timing, guts, and good timing. Let's unpack this, shall we?

Deciding to Come Out: Timing and Considerations

Assessing Readiness

First things first: are you ready? This isn't like deciding whether you're ready to dye your hair a funky color or try sushi for the first time. Coming out involves deep self-awareness and a hefty dose of bravery. It's essential to consider your emotional and relational stability. Are you emotionally equipped to handle a range of responses? Is your relationship on solid enough ground to withstand potential earthquakes? This stage is about checking your emotional barometer and ensuring you're not just reacting in the heat of the moment. It's okay if you decide the timing isn't right yet. This isn't a race; it's more like a personal journey where you get to set the pace.

Understanding Your Partner's Perspective

Next up, think about where your partner stands. Not literally, of course—I mean, understanding their current perceptions and beliefs about LGBTQ+ issues. This isn't about making assumptions based on their favorite reality shows or the books they read. It's about having honest, open pre-discussions that give you a sense of their views and values. Are they supportive of LGBTQ+ rights? How do they react to related news or events? This intel isn't just useful; it's crucial. It helps you tailor your approach in a way that speaks to them, respecting their feelings and potentially easing the pathway for your coming out.

Impact on Marriage

Let's talk impact. Coming out can shake the foundations of your marriage, affecting everything from day-to-day dynamics to long-term plans. It's like deciding to renovate your home while you're still living in it. Messy? Yes. Worth it? Absolutely—if done thoughtfully. Consider how your revelation might affect your shared responsibilities, intimacy, and social life. Will it bring you closer or build a wall? Timing this conversation around other significant life events can also be tricky. If you're already navigating major stresses like a big move, a new baby, or career changes, it might be wise to hold off until the waters are a bit calmer. It's all about finding the right moment when you're both ready to handle the waves together.

Seeking Professional Advice

And here's where a professional can come in handy. No, I'm not a professional juggler—though juggling emotions isn't far off. I'm talking about a therapist or counselor specializing in LGBTQ+ issues. Consulting a professional can provide a strategic plan tailored to your unique situation. They're like the GPS guiding you through uncharted territory, offering insights and coping strategies. Whether helping you craft your message or preparing you for possible reactions, their expertise can be a lifeline in a sea of uncertainty.

Interactive Element: Reflection Section

Let's pause for a bit of reflection. Grab a notebook and consider these prompts:

- On a scale of 1-10, how ready do you feel to come out, considering your emotional and relational stability?
- What conversations have you had with your partner that give you insights into their views on LGBTQ+ issues?
- How do you anticipate your coming out might impact your marriage in the short and long term?
- Have you considered seeking advice from a professional? What are your hopes and fears about this step?

Tackling these questions can help clarify your thoughts and feelings, providing a clearer roadmap for your coming out narrative. Remember, this chapter of your life doesn't need a spoiler alert. You're the author here; how and when you turn the page is entirely up to you. So take a deep breath, gather your support squad, and confidently step into your truth whenever you're ready. The spotlight's waiting, and it's yours to shine.

Strategies for Coming Out to a Heterosexual Partner

Imagine you've decided to renovate your shared life's kitchen—metaphorically. This renovation is your coming out. Now, where would you sit down to discuss the blueprint? Your choice of setting can be as crucial as the conversation itself. Think of a place where the walls don't just hold up your home but create a safe space, shielding both of you from the outside world's hustle and bustle. It could be your living room with the comfy couches, or perhaps during a quiet walk in your favorite park—somewhere you feel secure and private. This isn't the time for public declarations or over dinner in a crowded restaurant where the clatter of cutlery might drown out your words. A familiar, comforting environment can ease the intensity, making the space feel like only the two of you, ready to navigate this together.

Now, on to the dialogue—the heart of the matter. How do you put words to something that feels immensely personal yet pivotal? Start with honesty—simple, unadorned honesty. Phrases like, "I've been thinking a lot about who I am," or "I have something important about myself to share with you" set a tone of seriousness softened by vulnerability. These aren't just words; they're invitations for your partner to enter your inner world. It's crucial here to be clear but gentle, direct but kind. Avoid ambiguity, which can lead to confusion and speculation. You're not dropping clues for a treasure hunt; you're laying down a map to your truth. Express your feelings and what this identity means to you, but also reassure your partner that this revelation doesn't diminish your care for them. It's not about delivering a monologue; encourage them to voice their thoughts and feelings. This is a dialogue, a two-way street paved with words of truth and lanes of listening.

Preparing for their reactions is like setting up safety nets while tightrope walking. You hope not to fall, but it's best to be prepared if you do. Your partner's response could be supportive, neutral, or defensive. If they're supportive, that's great! But the ground might still shake a bit. If they're neutral or indifferent, encourage them to explore these feelings further in future conversations or through professional guidance. Defensive reactions, however, require a soft but firm approach—acknowledge their feelings and validate their confusion or hurt without compromising your truth. Remember, their first reactions aren't always last; emotions can evolve with understanding and time.

Finally, underline the concept of coming out as a process, not a one-off event. It's more series than movies—episodic and ongoing. This means continuous check-ins, open channels of communication, and perhaps more heart-to-hearts. Just as you wouldn't expect a single rain to water the garden forever, don't expect one conversation to cover everything. Nurture this part of your relationship with ongoing care, patience, and dialogue. Keep the lines open, the understanding flowing, and the assurance alive. This ongoing conversation ensures they comprehend and accept your identity and reinforce your commitment to each other, transforming challenges into stepping stones for a stronger relationship.

Handling Initial Reactions: What to Expect

Imagine the moment after you've shared your truth, the room still echoing with your last words. Now, picture your partner's face; it's like watching a silent movie where you must guess the ending. The range of emotions could stretch from shock and denial to acceptance and support, like someone traversing from the chilly shadows into warm sunlight. This spectrum can turn your ordinary living room into a stage of raw human emotions.

Shock and denial are often the knee-jerk reactions. Like someone who's just been woken from a deep sleep, your partner might need a moment—or many—to fully comprehend the news. They might even laugh it off or dismiss it as a joke, not out of malice but out of sheer unpreparedness. It's crucial here not to take these initial reactions to heart. Give them space to process this new information, like allowing someone time to adjust their eyes to a bright light after stepping out of the dark. Conversely, you might be met with immediate acceptance and support, a best-case scenario that feels like a warm embrace. Even then, remember, a cascade of questions might follow this initial support as the reality sets in over time.

Now, what should you do right after dropping your truth bomb? First, resist the urge to fill the silence. Let your partner process, think, and feel. This silence isn't empty; it's filled with the weight of your words, giving space for them to settle. Show empathy, acknowledge that this might be hard for them, and reassure them that you are still the person they loved yesterday—just be more honest now. Avoid language that assigns blame, like "You made me hide this," or anything that sounds remotely like an accusation. This moment is delicate; handle it with the care of someone holding a Ming vase.

Managing your emotions in this high-stress moment is like staying upright on a seesaw. It's about balance. You've just shared something incredibly personal, and the reaction you receive might stir a whirlpool of feelings inside you. Maintain your composure, even if the initial reaction isn't what you hoped for. This might mean taking deep breaths, reminding yourself why you came out, or even excusing yourself to collect your thoughts. It's okay to step back and breathe; resilience isn't about having a stiff upper lip but knowing when to pause and regroup.

Managing the long-term emotional responses becomes the next chapter as the days unfold. Whether the initial reactions were positive or not, the emotional dynamics can change. Like weather patterns, feelings can change, and storms may roll in unexpectedly. Continuous dialogue is key. Keep checking in, and encourage your partner to share their feelings, fears, and hopes as they evolve. This ongoing conversation isn't just about maintaining peace but deepening understanding and reinforcing your commitment to navigate this change together.

Navigating this emotional maze requires patience, a thick skin, and a heart ready to forgive and ask for forgiveness. Remember, reactions are not just about what's spoken. Watch for non-verbal cues, the unspoken words that often speak volumes. Are they withdrawing or leaning in? Are their arms crossed, or are their hands reaching for yours? These signs can guide how you continue the dialogue, offering insights into their emotional state beyond words.

As you move forward, remember that every reaction, every emotion, and every conversation is a step toward a deeper understanding. It's about finding a new normal where honesty paves the way for a richer, more authentic relationship. Whether the road is smooth or bumpy, the destination—a relationship built on truth and mutual respect—is well worth the journey. In this dance of disclosure and response, lead with your heart and let empathy guide you.

Supporting Your Partner Post-Coming Out

Imagine you just opened up a new chapter in your life's book—coming out to your partner. Now, think of the next steps as building a cozy reading nook for both of you to settle into this new chapter comfortably. It's about cushioning the space with understanding, lighting it up with resources, and ensuring there is enough room for open, honest dialogues.

Let's start with the resources. It's like suddenly realizing there are more chapters in the manual of life that you hadn't read before. For your partner, this might be their first encounter with the LGBTQ+ section of the library, and it's crucial to guide them to the right shelves. Consider introducing them to books that explain the basics of LGBTQ+ identities and experiences. Titles like "This is a Book for Parents of Gay Kids" by Dannielle Owens-Reid and Kristin Russo can be a gentle start. But books are just the beginning. Look into local or online support groups where they can listen to and share experiences with other heterosexual partners in mixed-orientation marriages. These groups can be invaluable, providing a sense of community and shared understanding. Counseling could also be helpful, providing professional guidance to navigate their thoughts and emotions about this new reality in their life together. Websites like Psychology Today can help find therapists who specialize in LGBTQ+ matters.

Now, about fostering those heart-to-heart dialogues. Encouraging an ongoing conversation is like keeping the lines in a play open and adaptable, where both characters genuinely listen and respond to each other. It's about creating a safe stage where fears, doubts, and hopes can be expressed freely without the script dictating every move. Ask open-ended questions like, "How do you feel about what I shared?" or "What can I do to help you through this?" It's also about you sharing your ongoing journey—this isn't a monologue. Share your daily feelings, experiences, and ups and downs as you navigate your identity. Sharing your experiences can make them more understandable and relatable, helping to build understanding.

Empathy, oh, the mighty glue that holds human connections together! In your interactions, try to step into your partner's shoes. They might be grappling with their identity shifts and societal expectations or worrying about what this means for the future you both envision. Show that you get it—it's not easy, and their feelings are valid. It's like saying, "I see this isn't easy on you, and that's okay. Let's figure this out together." It's about validating their process without pushing them to speed through their script. Sometimes, they might need a moment to be, absorb, and think. Give them that space, and let them know you're there when they're ready to talk.

Setting boundaries—now, that's an essential chapter in this new part of your journey. Healthy boundaries can help safeguard the emotional well-being of both of you. It's about knowing when to talk and give each other space. For instance, it might be setting a rule like not discussing this at family gatherings until you both are comfortable. Or deciding when you can have these discussions, ensuring neither of you needs to hold back feelings because it's not the 'right time.' It's also about respecting each other's privacy or processing time needs. Boundaries aren't walls; they're guidelines that help you both navigate this new terrain without losing yourselves.

By combining resources, open dialogue, empathy, and setting boundaries, you're building a strong foundation for your journeys. It's not just about adjusting to a new reality; it's about enhancing it and creating a meaningful chapter together, filled with understanding and mutual respect. Take it one step at a time, and keep strengthening your relationship with every shared moment, honest conversation, and heartfelt embrace.

Navigating Changes in Relationship Dynamics

Adjusting expectations within your marriage after coming out is like learning a new dance with an entirely different rhythm than what you're used to. It's not about mourning the loss of the old moves; instead, it's about embracing the opportunity to learn steps more in sync with who you both truly are. This adjustment phase can feel a bit like improvisational jazz at times. You both know the basics of music, but now the tune has changed slightly, and you're both listening intently to catch the beat. For starters, it's about recalibrating your expectations about your partnership's emotional and logistical aspects. This might mean rethinking your roles within the marriage, redefining what intimacy looks like for you, or even adjusting your long-term goals to suit your authentic versions of yourselves better. It's crucial during this time to maintain open lines of dialogue. Discuss openly what each of you envisions for the future, and be prepared for some of these visions to have shifted. Patience is your best friend; allow each other the space and grace to evolve within this refreshed dynamic.

Redefining emotional and physical intimacy is one of the most sensitive challenges you'll face during this transition. Intimacy in any relationship is the glue that binds partners together, creating a safe, shared space where vulnerabilities can be exposed without fear. In a mixed-orientation marriage, redefining this intimacy often involves deeply understanding each other's needs and comfort levels. Start by discussing what intimacy means to each of you now. You might find that emotional intimacy has become more crucial than physical intimacy, or you may discover new ways to express physical closeness that feel fulfilling and affirming for both partners. Remember, intimacy is not just about physical closeness; it's about feeling connected, seen, and valued by your partner in ways that resonate deeply with your emotional needs.

For couples with children, co-parenting while dealing with changing marital dynamics adds another challenge. It's paramount to ensure that the foundation you set for your children remains stable and secure, even if your relationship with your spouse transforms. Open communication about the changes in your relationship is essential. Depending on their age and understanding, children may have questions or concerns. Straightforwardly address these changes, ensuring that the conversation is framed in a way that emphasizes love, respect, and honesty. Discuss with your partner how you will handle parental responsibilities and ensure that both of you agree regarding the values and principles you want to impart to your children. The goal is to maintain a united front as parents, providing a nurturing environment filled with unconditional support.

Looking toward the future involves a mixture of practical and emotional planning. It's about building on the new foundation you've established in your honest discussions and shared experiences post-coming out. Consider what adjustments need to be made regarding living arrangements or financial planning. Perhaps the physical space you share needs reconfiguring to reflect the current dynamics better. Alternatively, it's time to revisit financial goals and responsibilities to ensure they align with your individual and collective needs. Planning for the future also means considering how you'll continue to support each other's growth and happiness. Set time aside to discuss your aspirations, fears, and all the exciting possibilities that lie ahead. This isn't just about logistical planning; it's about dreaming together, reimagining your joint path, and taking deliberate steps toward a future that embraces your truths.

Navigating these changes won't always be straightforward, and there might be moments of discordance. Still, with each step taken in honesty and love, you'll find that a new harmony is possible—a melody that plays true to who you both are, individually and together. As you adjust, redefine, and plan, keep communication open, respect each other's feelings, and commit to navigating this new phase with openness and understanding.

When Coming Out Doesn't Go as Planned: Next Steps

Sometimes, despite your best-laid plans, the script takes a turn you didn't see coming. You've gathered your courage, rehearsed your lines, set the stage for a supportive reveal, and yet, the reaction you receive might throw you off your feet. It could be a partner's denial, a wave of anger, or even a storm of emotions leading them to suggest separation. In these moments, it can feel like your world is spinning out of control. But remember, this isn't the closing act; it's just a twist in the plot, and there are ways to navigate these choppy waters.

Handling these adverse outcomes first requires taking a deep breath. Yes, a deep, soul-filling breath. It's about grounding yourself during this emotional tornado and protecting your core. Begin by acknowledging the pain without letting it consume you. It's okay to feel hurt, confused, or angry. These are natural responses to unexpected reactions. However, it's crucial not to retaliate or close off. Instead, approach the situation with a mindset geared toward understanding and resolution. If the conversation becomes too heated or you feel overwhelmed, it's perfectly okay to pause. "Let's take a moment to process this" is a simple way to hit the pause button, giving both of you space to breathe and collect your thoughts.

Seeking external support plays a vital role in navigating this phase. Turn to friends, family members, or support groups who stand by the values of love and acceptance. These folks will offer you a shoulder to lean on, an understanding ear, or even just sit with you in silence, offering their presence as a comfort. Remember, these sources of support should uplift and not influence you negatively against your partner. It's about finding a balance where you can express your frustrations and fears without fueling fires at home. Additionally, professional support from counselors who specialize in LGBTQ+ issues can provide you with strategies to manage these conversations with your partner and help you both navigate this rocky phase with more understanding and less conflict.

Then there's the part about reassessing your goals—both personally and jointly. It's like taking a step back to look at your relationship map to see where you are and where you want to go. This reassessment doesn't mean giving up on previous plans, but it might involve tweaking them to fit the current reality of your relationship better. Ask yourself, "What do we want from our relationship moving forward?" and "How can we redefine our paths so they feel more aligned with who we are today?" This conversation can be tough but think of it as an opportunity to build a future that resonates more authentically with your needs and desires.

Self-care is your anchor through all of this. It's easy to get lost in the storm and neglect your well-being, but remember, you can't pour from an empty cup. Develop a self-care routine that nourishes your mind, body, and spirit. Whether journaling your thoughts, meditating, engaging in physical activities, or simply doing more of what makes you happy—make time for it. Resilience is built by enduring hard times and fostering an environment where you can thrive, even amid challenges. This resilience isn't just about bouncing back; it's about growing stronger and more grounded in who you are, regardless of the turbulence around you.

Navigating the aftermath of a coming-out that didn't go as planned is undeniably tough. It tests your strength, resilience, and capacity for forgiveness toward yourself and your partner. Yet, through this testing ground, there's also profound potential for growth and deeper understanding. By leaning on support, reassessing your shared goals, and prioritizing self-care, you equip yourself with the tools to survive this chapter and eventually thrive, crafting a true narrative.

As this chapter wraps up, remember what we've covered. It's about navigating the unexpected with grace, seeking support to steady your ship, recharting your course with renewed understanding, and caring deeply for yourself through every step. As we turn the page to the next chapter, let's carry forward this resilience and openness, ready to explore further depths of our relationships and ourselves.

THREE

Emotional and Psychological Support

Let's face it: navigating a mixed-orientation marriage can sometimes feel like trying to solve a Rubik's Cube in the dark. It's complex, often confusing, and requires a good sense of humor and patience! But here's the kicker: just like mastering any puzzle, having the right tools and guidance can turn a seemingly impossible task into a series of manageable steps. This chapter is about equipping you with the emotional and psychological support tools that make this journey more navigable and enriching for you and your partner. So, buckle up! We're about to dive into the world of therapy, self-discovery, and personal growth that doesn't require you to sit cross-legged on a mountain (unless that's your thing, of course).

Individual Therapy Options for Each Partner

Identifying Needs

First off, let's talk about identifying your needs. Think of this as your mental shopping list. What is it that you're looking for in therapy?

This isn't about being selfish; it's about being self-aware. For the partner coming out, perhaps you're seeking support in navigating your identity, or maybe you need help managing the stress of new changes in your life and relationship. For the heterosexual partner, perhaps you're grappling with uncertainty or need tools to help adjust to the new dynamics in your marriage. Pinpointing these needs isn't always straightforward, so it might help to start with broad feelings or challenges you're experiencing and work your way into the specifics. Think of it as beginning with a full cart and then deciding what you need for the week ahead.

Different Therapeutic Approaches

Now, onto the therapy menu. Yes, there are different flavors; no, one size does not fit all. Cognitive-behavioral therapy (CBT) is like your practical, problem-solving friend. It focuses on identifying and changing negative thought patterns and behaviors. It's pretty handy for tackling issues like anxiety or depression that might crop up in your relationship dynamics. Then there's psychodynamic therapy—think of it as the deep diver. It aims to unearth deeper emotional roots and past experiences that could influence your current relationship. This can be particularly enlightening if your marital issues are linked to deeper, more complex emotional patterns.

Narrative therapy, on the other hand, is like having a scriptwriter in your head. It encourages you to reframe your life's story in a way that empowers you, viewing problems as separate from yourself. This can be especially liberating when dealing with identity and role changes in your marriage. Each of these therapies offers unique tools and insights, so consider what might resonate most with your style and specific needs.

Finding LGBTQ+ Affirmative Therapists

The quest for the right therapist can feel like dating. You want someone who gets you, respects you, and can genuinely contribute to your growth. When it comes to mixed-orientation marriages, it's crucial to find therapists who are not just inclusive but affirmatively trained in LGBTQ+ issues. This ensures they're both culturally competent and sensitive to your specific challenges. Websites like the Psychology Today Therapist Directory can be great starting points. They allow you to filter your search by issues, sexuality, and even languages spoken. Remember, it's okay to shop around. Think of the first session as a casual coffee date. You're there to see if you click, so don't be afraid to ask about their experience with mixed-orientation couples and their approach to therapy.

Leveraging Therapy for Personal Growth

Therapy isn't just about fixing problems; it's about cultivating a flourishing life within and outside your marriage. It's like hiring a personal trainer for your mental and emotional well-being. Beyond coping with the immediate challenges of your marriage, therapy can be a space for profound personal growth and self-discovery. It can help you enhance your communication skills, increase your emotional intelligence, and even boost your overall resilience. Plus, your relationship will likely reap the benefits as you grow individually. After all, when you bring the best version of yourself to the table, the relationship feast is all the more delicious.

Interactive Element: Reflection Section

Take a moment to jot down your thoughts:

- What specific emotional or psychological challenges are you currently facing in your marriage?
- Which therapeutic approach resonates most with you, and why?
- Have you considered seeking an LGBTQ+ affirmative therapist? What qualities would you look for in a therapist?

Thinking about these questions can help you navigate therapy more confidently and clearly, ensuring you find support that fits your needs and goals.

As we wrap up this section, consider therapy a remedy and a proactive step toward a healthier, happier you—and a more robust, more resilient marriage. Whether you're dealing with identity issues, marital challenges, or just the daily stresses of life, remember that seeking help is a sign of strength, not weakness. So, give yourself a pat on the back; you're taking steps to improve your life and deepen and enrich your relationship. And that, my friend, is worth celebrating.

The Importance of Couples Counseling

Think of couples counseling as your relationship's tune-up session. You know, when you take your car into the shop, not because it's broken down, but because you want to keep it purring like a kitten. That's exactly what couples counseling can do for your marriage. It's a space to roll up your sleeves, pop the hood on your relationship, and work together to keep things running smoothly. Particularly in a mixed-orientation marriage, where the road can sometimes feel bumpy, having a skilled mechanic, or in this case, a therapist, can make all the difference.

Facilitating Communication

Let's start with communication, which is the engine of any relationship. In couples counseling, you get to learn the art of maintenance. This isn't about patching up and moving on; it's about understanding how to communicate effectively. For instance, counselors often use techniques that help each partner express their feelings and needs without turning the garage into a battleground. Imagine being given the tools to say what's on your mind and do it in a way your partner hears and understands you. It's about turning monologues into dialogues and ensuring no one's emotions are left idling in the background.

Addressing Marital Challenges

Now, onto the nuts and bolts of specific marital challenges. Mixed-orientation marriages might face unique issues, like discrepancies in sexual desires and expectations. In counseling, you and your partner get to address this head-on. It's like recalibrating your GPS to ensure you're both navigating the same route. A counselor can help you explore these sensitive topics in a safe, structured environment that focuses on finding solutions that work for both of you. Whether adjusting your intimacy levels or renegotiating boundaries, the goal is to ensure that both partners feel comfortable and respected in their journey together.

Enhancing Relationship Resilience

Building resilience within your marriage is another critical aspect of couples counseling. Think of this as your relationship's safety features—airbags and seatbelts. Life will inevitably throw some curveballs your way, and resilience helps you handle the impact without veering off the road. Counselors work with you to develop strategies to manage stress and conflict. These might include techniques for de-escalation during heated arguments, exercises to strengthen your emotional connection, or even just regular check-ins to gauge the health of your relationship. This way, when you hit a pothole, you're better equipped to handle it without causing damage.

Case Examples

Let's look at some real-life pit stops where couples counseling has made a significant difference. Picture Sarah and Bailey, a couple who entered counseling feeling like they were constantly at odds because of their differing sexual orientations. Through sessions focused on communication, they learned how to express their needs and listen to each other without judgment. They established a new understanding of intimacy that respected their boundaries and brought them closer together.

Then there's Jordan and Bailey, who found that stress from external pressures about their mixed-orientation marriage was starting to affect their relationship. Through counseling, they developed strategies to support each other during interactions with unsupportive family members and to reinforce their united front. This enhanced their resilience and deepened their trust and commitment to each other.

Each of these examples shines a light on how couples counseling doesn't just patch up relationships; it rebuilds them stronger and more ready to handle whatever the road ahead has in store. Whether it's enhancing communication, tackling specific marital challenges, or building resilience, the journey through counseling is one of mutual growth and reinforced connection. So, consider this chapter your reminder that sometimes, seeking help is the best way to keep your relationship engine running smoothly, ensuring that both of you can enjoy the ride, no matter where the road may lead.

Dealing with Guilt and Shame in Mixed-Orientation Marriages

Guilt and shame, those pesky uninvited guests at the dinner party of our lives, can often take a front seat in mixed-orientation marriages. You might feel guilt for not fulfilling societal or personal expectations of what a 'normal' marriage looks like, or perhaps you're wrestling with shame stemming from ingrained cultural or religious beliefs about sexuality. Understanding where these feelings come from is like shining a flashlight into the darker corners of your emotional attic—it's not just about cleaning out old cobwebs but about understanding why they gathered there in the first place.

The origins of guilt and shame in mixed-orientation marriages are as multifaceted as the emotions themselves. Society, with its knack for setting up a 'standard' model of marriage, often doesn't know where to place relationships that don't fit the mold. This societal pressure can make you feel like you must constantly justify your love or your partnership's validity. Then there are personal expectations—maybe you've always pictured your life a certain way or absorbed the idea that being a good spouse means adhering to specific norms. And let's not forget the role of religious beliefs, which, for many, can be a source of deep-rooted ideas about morality and sin, particularly around issues of sexuality.

So, how do you start clearing out these emotional cobwebs? Cognitive restructuring is a technique that is your new best friend. Here's the scoop: it involves identifying and challenging the negative thought patterns that fuel your feelings of guilt or shame. For instance, if you find yourself thinking, "I'm failing as a spouse because our marriage doesn't look like everyone else's," you would challenge this by asking, "Says who?" and "What does a 'successful' marriage truly look like?" It's about rewriting the narrative in your head so that it's less about societal scripts and more about what makes your relationship genuinely fulfilling and happy.

Managing shame can be tricky because it often resembles a shadow following you around, coloring how you see yourself and your life. Engaging in vulnerability exercises can be incredibly powerful here. This involves opening up about your shame in a safe environment, perhaps with a therapist or a trusted friend. Sharing what you feel ashamed about diminishes its power—suddenly, the monster in the closet isn't so scary once you turn on the light. Implementing principles from shame-resilience theory, such as those proposed by Brené Brown, can also be transformative. Brown suggests that recognizing your triggers, practicing critical awareness about why you feel what you do, reaching out for support, and speaking about your experiences can all build your resilience against shame.

And speaking of support, let's talk about the cavalry that can help you in this battle against guilt and shame. Support groups and resources specifically tailored to mixed-orientation marriages can be invaluable. These groups provide a safe space to share your experiences and feelings without judgment, surrounded by others who understand exactly what you're going through. It's like having a team there to cheer you on and pass you water when the marathon gets tough. Organizations such as the Straight Spouse Network or local LGBTQ+ centers often offer support groups that can be both a lifeline and a valuable resource.

Navigating the complex emotions of guilt and shame in your marriage isn't about suppressing these feelings or pretending they don't exist. Instead, it's about understanding their origins, actively working through them, and seeking the support that reminds you— you're not alone. As you continue engaging with these strategies and resources, you'll likely find that guilt and shame become lighter, not because the situations have changed but because you've equipped yourself with the tools to handle them more effectively. As you do this work, remember that every step forward, no matter how small, is a step toward a healthier, happier you and a stronger, more resilient marriage.

Maintaining Emotional Intimacy After Coming Out

Rebuilding Trust

Trust, that invisible thread that holds the fabric of relationships together, can become somewhat frayed after one partner comes out. It's not that the love has diminished or the commitment has wavered; it's just that the relationship dynamics have shifted, sometimes unexpectedly. Rebuilding trust isn't about returning to how things were but moving forward to how things can be even better and stronger. Think of it as updating the software of your relationship—

it might disrupt the normal flow for a bit, but it's essential for smoother functioning in the long run.

One of the first steps in this updating process is open communication. This goes beyond discussing the weather or who needs to pick up the groceries. It's about sharing your fears, insecurities, and expectations. It's about being honest when you're hurting and receptive when your partner shares their vulnerabilities. This level of openness doesn't just patch up trust; it rebuilds it layer by layer. Another strategy is consistency. Be it in your words or actions, consistency sends a signal to your partner that they can rely on you, that you're there, steadfast. This could be as simple as always showing up on time for dinner dates or as deep as consistently respecting boundaries that you've both set.

Building new trust rituals can also be incredibly powerful. These are actions that you consistently engage in that reinforce trust. Maybe it's a weekly check-in where you both share one thing you appreciated about each other that week or perhaps it's a daily text or note just to say, "I'm thinking of you." Small or significant rituals become the new pillars on which your renewed trust is built, ensuring the foundation of your relationship is robust and resilient.

New Forms of Intimacy

Navigating intimacy after coming out can feel like learning a new language. The words and gestures you used to express love and closeness need some updating. This is where exploring new forms of emotional intimacy can play a transformative role. Shared hobbies, for instance, can be a wonderful way to reconnect. Whether it's cooking, hiking, painting, or anything you enjoy, shared hobbies create a space for laughter, creativity, and connection, away from the pressures of navigating a mixed-orientation relationship.

Deep conversations are another avenue to explore. These aren't just any conversations; they're the kind where you dive into each other's hopes, dreams, fears, and the big "whys" of life. They require time, openness, and a willingness to be vulnerable—qualities that profoundly foster intimacy. Mutual support, too, is a cornerstone of emotional intimacy. Being each other's cheerleader, confidante, and safe space in a challenging world strengthens your bond, reinforcing the "us against the world" team spirit that every enduring relationship needs.

Regular Check-ins

Think of regular emotional check-ins as the relationship equivalent of a health check-up. They help catch minor issues before they become big problems, ensuring that the emotional health of your relationship remains in tip-top shape. These check-ins can be structured (like setting a specific time each week to talk about how you both are feeling) or more spontaneous (like taking a moment during a quiet evening to ask, "How are we doing?"). The key here is regularity and sincerity. It's not about going through the motions; it's about genuinely wanting to know and understand your partner's emotional state and sharing your own.

During these check-ins, it's important to celebrate the wins, not just discuss challenges. Share what you love about each other, express gratitude for the small acts of kindness, and reaffirm your commitment to navigating this journey together. These positive affirmations, coupled with constructive discussions on areas that need attention, can significantly enhance the quality of your emotional connection, keeping the lines of communication open and fluid.

Professional Guidance

Sometimes, the best way to navigate shifts in intimacy is to call in the experts. Professional guidance from a therapist, especially one well-versed in LGBTQ+ dynamics, can be invaluable. They can offer new perspectives and strategies you might have yet to consider, acting as a neutral facilitator in discussions that might be too difficult to tackle alone. Whether working through emotional blockages, exploring new dimensions of intimacy, or just strengthening communication, a therapist can guide you through these complexities in a structured, supportive environment.

This professional input can be constructive when emotions are raw, or the usual connecting methods fall short. It can help unpack the underlying emotions, foster deeper understanding, and provide practical tools for building intimacy in ways that resonate with both partners. Essentially, it helps translate the language of love in ways each partner can understand and appreciate, smoothing the path toward a richer, more fulfilling relationship.

As we continue to explore the nuances of emotional and psychological support in mixed-orientation marriages, remember that each step forward, no matter how small, is a step toward a deeper connection and understanding. It's about building a relationship that thrives on trust, intimacy, and mutual respect, equipped with the tools to navigate any challenge that comes your way.

Anxiety and Depression: Support and Compelling Strategies

Navigating a mixed-orientation marriage can sometimes feel like you're trying to juggle while balancing on a tightrope—it's no wonder that feelings of anxiety and depression can sneak in. Don't get me wrong; a little bit of stress is as normal as forgetting where you put your keys, but when these feelings start to feel more like uninvited house guests that won't leave, it might be time to address them head-on. So, let's unpack these emotional suitcases together, shall we?

Recognizing Symptoms

First up, recognizing the signs. Anxiety might show up as that pesky knot in your stomach that doesn't seem to untangle, no matter how many episodes of your favorite sitcom you watch. Or it could be that your mind is racing faster than a caffeinated hamster on a wheel, making it tough to catch your breath or even a good night's sleep. Depression, on the other hand, might feel like you're constantly wearing a heavy coat that you can't take off. It could be a persistent sadness, a loss of interest in things you used to love—like turning down a karaoke night with friends, or even just feeling tired all the time despite resting. These emotional and physical cues are your body's way of saying, "Hey, something's up," and it's important to listen.

Professional Help

When these feelings start to turn your daily life into a slog, reaching out for professional help can be a game-changer. It's like calling in a lifeguard when you feel like drowning. Psychiatrists and therapists can offer different types of support. In contrast, psychiatrists can prescribe medications to help manage symptoms of severe anxiety or depression. Therapists provide a safe space to talk through your feelings and start untangling those emotional knots. Both paths aim to get you back to feeling like yourself again, and there's no shame in taking medication if that's what helps. It's just another tool in your emotional toolkit that can help clear the fog so you can enjoy the view again.

Self-Help Techniques

But what about those days when you're just feeling a bit off? Self-help techniques can be your go-to for mild symptoms and general mental upkeep. Think of these as your daily emotional exercises. Mindfulness, for instance, is like giving your brain a mini-vacation. Apps like Headspace or Calm offer guided meditations that can help you center your thoughts and ease anxiety. Exercise, too, can be incredibly effective. It's not just about getting fit; it's about flushing out the stress hormones and getting those feel-good endorphins pumping. Even a quick walk around the block can lift your spirits.

And let's not forget about journaling—it's like conversing with yourself on paper. Sometimes, writing down your thoughts can help you see things more clearly and feel lighter.

Community and Online Support

Lastly, remember that you're not alone in this. There's a whole community out there who understands exactly what you're going through and can offer a shoulder to lean on or even just a listening ear. Online forums, support groups, and social media platforms can connect you with people in similar situations. Websites like Reddit have threads dedicated to mental health and LGBTQAI+ issues where you can share your experiences and tips in a supportive environment. Local LGBTQAI+ centers often offer support groups for mixed-orientation couples, providing a space to discuss challenges and celebrate victories with others who get it.

By recognizing the signs of anxiety and depression, seeking professional help when needed, employing self-help techniques, and tapping into community support, you can start to take back control of your emotional health. Whether through medication, meditation, or conversation, the goal is to find what works for you to navigate your marriage and life more easily and joyfully. So, take a deep breath, pick up the right tools, and step forward into a brighter, lighter path.

Building Resilience and Emotional Strength

Resilience in a mixed-orientation marriage? Think of it as the relationship's immune system—keeping you healthy and thriving, no matter what germs life throws. It's about bouncing back from challenges and changes, not just unscathed, but stronger and wiser. Why is it crucial? Imagine navigating a boat in choppy waters without knowing how to steer through the waves. You're going to get pretty wet, right? Resilience equips you both with the skills to steer through life's storms, keeping your boat afloat and sailing smoothly.

One powerful strategy for building resilience is embracing a growth mindset. This is all about seeing challenges not as roadblocks but as stepping stones to learning and development. It's turning the "Why is this happening to us?" into "What can we learn from this?" For instance, when disagreements arise, a growth mindset helps you view them as opportunities to deepen your understanding of each other rather than battles to win. This mindset encourages you to ask questions, seek understanding, and embrace the idea that you are ever-evolving beings, continually learning to love each other better.

Setting realistic expectations is another key to resilience. Let's be honest: expecting your partner to read your mind or always know the right thing to say is like expecting a cat to bark—it's just not going to happen. Understanding and accepting each other's strengths and limitations helps prevent disappointment and fosters a culture of mutual support and forgiveness. It's about knowing that your partner is human, just like you, and that mistakes are part of the journey. By setting realistic expectations, you both can navigate life's ups and downs without undue pressure, making your relationship more resilient to external stresses.

Fostering a sense of shared purpose can also significantly strengthen your resilience. This means connecting over common goals and values that transcend the everyday aspects of your relationship. Whether it's a shared passion for travel, a joint business venture, or a mutual commitment to family or community service, having a shared purpose unites you, giving you a reason to fight through tough times together. It's like having a team jersey that reminds you both what team you're on, especially when the game gets tough.

Let's sprinkle some real-life magic into our discussion with stories of couples who've navigated their mixed-orientation marriages with grace and resilience. Take Ellie and Sam, for instance. When Sam came out as transgender, the couple faced not just personal adjustments but also external pressures and prejudices. However, through open communication, a commitment to understanding each other's needs, and a shared goal of advocating for transgender rights, they strengthened their bond and became role models for their community. Their story highlights how resilience can transform challenges into powerful opportunities for growth and impact.

Or consider Maya and Joe. After Maya came out as bisexual, the couple struggled with insecurity and jealousy. But instead of letting these challenges tear them apart, they used them as catalysts for growth. They attended workshops on trust, read books on open communication, and set aside time each week to openly discuss their feelings and fears. Over time, these practices helped them build a stronger, more trusting relationship, turning their initial struggles into testimonies of their commitment and resilience.

These stories underline the transformative power of resilience in mixed-orientation marriages. By embracing a growth mindset, setting realistic expectations, fostering a shared purpose, and learning from each challenge, couples can survive and thrive, turning their unique challenges into sources of strength and joy.

As we close this chapter on emotional and psychological support, remember that the tools and strategies discussed here are theoretical concepts and practical, actionable steps that can significantly enhance your relationship. From navigating the complexities of therapy and counseling to tackling the emotional challenges of guilt, shame, anxiety, and depression to ultimately building resilience and emotional strength, each section has equipped you with the knowledge not just to face but embrace the challenges of your mixed-orientation marriage. As you turn the page to the next chapter, carry forward these insights with a spirit of hope and a commitment to continuous growth, both individually and as a couple.

FOUR

Legal and Financial Considerations

Navigating the legal maze of a mixed-orientation marriage can sometimes feel like you're trying to do a crossword puzzle with a blunt pencil. It's tricky and sometimes frustrating, but the satisfaction when you get it right! This chapter is your sharper pencil, helping you sketch out the rights, protections, and legal nuances that are part of the unique artistry of your marriage. Buckle up; we're diving into the fine print with a splash of humor and heart.

Understanding Your Legal Rights and Protections

Awareness of Legal Rights

First things first, let's talk about your legal rights. Knowing these is like having a good map before you embark on a road trip—it's essential. In mixed-orientation marriages, your rights are primarily defined by anti-discrimination laws and marriage equality acts. These laws are the guardrails that keep you safe on your journey, ensuring you're treated fairly, whether applying for a loan, renting a house, or visiting your partner in the hospital. For instance, the U.S. Supreme

Court's decision in Obergefell v. Hodges was a landmark victory that legalized same-sex marriage nationwide, ensuring that no state can deny marriage licenses or refuse to recognize the marriage based on the couple's gender.

But it's not just about being able to marry. These laws protect you from employment, housing, and discrimination, so understanding them is crucial. It's like knowing which tools are in your toolbox and how to use them if you need to fix something. Knowledge is power; in this case, it's the power to protect your rights and your family.

Navigating Legal Systems

Navigating the legal system when your rights are challenged can feel like trying to solve a Rubik's cube—it's complex, and every move counts. This is where having legal representation can make a big difference. Think of lawyers as your navigators in the legal world; they know the shortcuts, the pitfalls, and the rules of the road. Whether you're facing discrimination, sorting out adoption rights, or dealing with inheritance issues, a good attorney can help you navigate these challenges more smoothly.

Moreover, don't overlook the power of advocacy groups. These organizations are like your roadside assistance. Groups like the ACLU or Lambda Legal fight tirelessly for the rights of LGBTQ+ individuals and can offer guidance, support, and sometimes even legal representation. They're also great at pushing for changes to laws that make everyone's journey a bit smoother.

State-Specific Laws

State-specific laws can be different from one state to another. Each state has its recipe for a dish called 'legal rights stew'—some are more generous with the spices, and others, not so much. For example, some states have robust protections against discrimination based on sexual orientation and gender identity, while in others, these protections are thinner or non-existent. This is why knowing the laws in your state—or any state you plan to move to—is crucial. Websites like the Human Rights Campaign (HRC) provide detailed maps and breakdowns of state-specific laws affecting LGBTQ+ individuals and can be invaluable.

Case Law Examples

To understand how these laws play out in real life, let's look at some key legal cases. These cases are like stories from the front lines, showing us the struggles and triumphs in the fight for equality. For example, the Windsor v. United States case struck down parts of the Defense of Marriage Act (DOMA) and paved the way for recognizing same-sex marriages at the federal level. Then there's the Masterpiece Cakeshop case, which balanced anti-discrimination protections with religious freedoms, a reminder of the ongoing challenges in ensuring equal rights for all.

These cases do more than tell a story; they set precedents that impact lives, shaping the legal framework under which mixed-orientation couples live and love. They remind us that while the road to equality can be bumpy, each victory brings us closer to a world where love is celebrated in all its forms.

Navigating the legal aspects of a mixed-orientation marriage might not be the easiest journey you'll take, but with the right map, a good guide, and a dash of knowledge, it's certainly one that you can manage with confidence. Remember, understanding your rights isn't just about protecting yourself; it's about paving the way for a smoother, more secure path for the love you share. So, take this knowledge, tuck it into your back pocket, and walk forward, knowing you can handle whatever the legal world throws.

Financial Planning and Security in Transition

Managing finances during a transitional phase in your marriage, such as when one partner comes out, can sometimes feel like trying to assemble a piece of IKEA furniture without the instructions. Sure, It can be daunting, but with the right tools and a bit of savvy planning, you'll piece together a financial plan that stands up and supports the unique structure of your mixed-orientation marriage.

Budgeting During Transition

Let's start with budgeting—it's like the foundation of your financial house. Changes in your relationship dynamics can lead to changes in financial dynamics, too. Maybe one partner decides to step back from work to figure things out, or perhaps there are new costs associated with counseling or healthcare to consider. Whatever the case, revisiting your budget is crucial. Begin with a clear, honest discussion about your current financial situation. Lay all your cards on the table: income, expenses, debt, and savings. From there, identify your new financial goals and priorities. Maybe you need to tighten the dining out budget to afford a couples retreat, or it's time to start a separate fund for potential legal expenses. Tools like budgeting apps can be tremendously helpful here, allowing you to track your spending in real time and adjust on the fly. It's like having a financial advisor in your pocket, one that reminds you gently about your spending goals.

Securing Financial Independence

Now, onto a slightly more challenging topic—securing financial independence. This is key, especially in scenarios where the future of the marriage is uncertain. It's about ensuring that both partners can financially stand independently, no matter what happens. Start by evaluating your earning capabilities and potential. It might be time to consider additional training or education to enhance job prospects. Opening individual bank accounts is also a practical step if you haven't already done so. It's not about setting the stage for a breakup; it's about empowering each partner financially, which can bring a sense of security and equality to the relationship. Think of it as having your safety nets in place, which allow you to contribute to the marriage from a place of strength, not dependency.

Financial Advisors

Consulting with financial advisors who specialize in handling cases for mixed-orientation marriages can be a game-changer. These professionals are familiar with your situation's unique challenges and opportunities. They can guide you in everything from restructuring your investments to planning for tax implications that might arise from any changes in your marital status. Consider it like having a seasoned guide while trekking through unfamiliar territory. They can help chart the course, point out the pitfalls, and ensure you make the most informed financial decisions during your transition.

Insurance and Benefits

Finally, let's tackle insurance and benefits—a world that's as complex as any. If one partner is coming out, affecting your marital status, you might need to review and renegotiate the terms of your life, health, and other insurance policies. For instance, understanding how to divide benefits like health or life insurance beneficiaries is crucial if a separation is on the cards. Sitting down with a benefits coordinator or an insurance agent becomes essential. They can help you understand the implications of any changes and guide you in making adjustments to ensure that both partners remain adequately covered. It's about ensuring that while your relationship's emotional aspects might be in flux, your insurance safety net remains intact and responsive to your needs.

Navigating financial planning and security during a marriage transition is undoubtedly complex. Still, with thoughtful budgeting, a focus on financial independence, the guidance of specialized financial advisors, and careful insurance and benefits management, you can create a stable financial environment that supports both partners through whatever changes may come. It's about building financial security and a foundation of trust and support that can help weather any storms on the horizon.

Navigating Divorce and Custody Issues

When the shared life you've built starts resembling a DIY project gone awry, understanding the ins and outs of divorce proceedings can feel as crucial as finding the instruction manual. In mixed-orientation marriages, just like any others, the process can get tangled with emotional, legal, and practical threads that need careful unraveling. Let's start with the legal nuances of divorce in these unique situations. It's not just about who gets the coffee maker; it's about navigating a process that respects both partners' dignity and individual rights. The legal framework here isn't just complicated due to emotional factors; it often includes layers of laws that weren't created with mixed-orientation couples in mind. This is where knowing the specific challenges and considerations that apply to your situation becomes crucial. For instance, if one partner came out during the marriage, how does that impact divorce grounds in states requiring them? The answers aren't always straightforward, but they're essential in handling the process fairly and sensitively.

Transitioning to custody and co-parenting, the plot thickens. Here, the priority shifts to the well-being of any children involved. This isn't about splitting assets; it's about crafting a plan that supports the kids' best interests while respecting each parent's rights and roles. Effective co-parenting strategies often start with open communication and a commitment to cooperation. It's like being teammates in a relay race – working together smoothly is more important than who goes the fastest. Structured agreements that outline parenting schedules, decision-making processes, and conflict-resolution plans are tools that can keep things running smoothly. It's also about flexibility—being willing to adjust the plan as your kids grow and their needs change, ensuring that the parenting plan evolves as dynamically as your family.

Now, let's talk assets. Dividing them can stir up more drama than a season finale cliffhanger. Whether it's the family home, savings accounts, or that painting you both love, dividing assets equitably is key. This doesn't always mean a 50/50 split. Instead, it's about equitable distribution based on factors like each partner's financial contributions, earning capacity, and the needs of any children. It's about fairness and respect, ensuring that both partners feel that their tangible and intangible contributions are acknowledged. Sometimes, you might even decide to keep some assets joint for practical reasons, like maintaining a home for the children until they reach adulthood. Think of it as less about cutting the pie into exactly equal slices and more about making sure everyone has enough pie to feel satisfied.

Legal support, ever so crucial, is the backbone of navigating divorce and custody effectively. Specialized legal support, familiar with the intricacies of family law as it applies to mixed-orientation marriages, can be the difference between a process filled with pitfalls and one that leads to a fair, respectful resolution. A good attorney doesn't just guide you through the legalities; they advocate for your rights and interests, helping to steer negotiations and, if necessary, court proceedings in a direction that protects what's most important to you. Whether negotiating custody or dividing assets, having a legal expert in your corner is like having a seasoned guide through a challenging hike—they know the terrain, the shortcuts, and how to navigate the obstacles so you can focus on moving forward.

Navigating divorce and custody issues in the context of a mixed-orientation marriage is undoubtedly complex. But with a clear understanding of the legal nuances, a commitment to effective co-parenting, a fair approach to asset division, and the right legal support, it's possible to manage this transition with integrity and respect for everyone involved. It's about taking each step thoughtfully, armed with the right information and support, to reshape the structure of your family in a way that supports the well-being and happiness of all members. As you continue to navigate these challenges, remember that while the road may be rough, the strength and resilience you bring to the journey can lead to new beginnings and positive outcomes for everyone involved.

Estate Planning and Inheritance Issues

Let's face it: talking about wills, estate taxes, and all that jazz might remind you of that one guest at a party who just can't stop talking about their bizarre hobbies. But just like that guest, there's something valuable beneath the surface chatter. When you're navigating a mixed-orientation marriage, getting your estate planning dialed in is like making sure your parachute is packed correctly before skydiving. It's essential, reassuring, and can save a lot of hassle down the road.

Drafting Wills

Starting with wills—think of a will as your ultimate 'to-do' list after you've left the party early. It's your voice from beyond, detailing who gets what and who looks after the cat. For mixed-orientation couples, ensuring that both partners' wishes are respected after one passes away is crucial, especially if the legal recognition of your relationship might be questioned. It's not just about who gets the antique lamp when drafting wills. It's about making clear legal statements regarding your mutual wishes. This can provide peace of mind and prevent potential legal battles with family members who may not recognize or support your relationship.

The key here is specificity and clarity. Detailing each item or asset, who it goes to, and any special instructions can help avoid ambiguity that could lead to disputes. Also, consider including a letter of explanation with your will that outlines your reasoning. This can be particularly helpful in smoothing any bumps that arise from unexpected decisions, like leaving something significant to a non-family member.

Inheritance Laws

Moving on to the thrilling world of inheritance laws. These can be as tricky as solving a crossword puzzle where half the clues are in another language. Inheritance laws vary significantly from place to place, and in some areas, they still need to catch up with the concept of mixed-orientation marriages. This can lead to scenarios where, without proper planning, a surviving partner might not automatically inherit assets or, worse, might find themselves in legal battles with family members.

It's vital to understand the specific inheritance laws in your area, especially regarding how they apply to non-traditional relationships. In some regions, additional steps may be necessary to ensure that assets are passed on according to your wishes, like setting up trusts or designating beneficiaries explicitly in all financial and pension plans. Remember, the goal here isn't just to plan for the inevitable but to do so in a way that protects your partner and ensures that your wishes are carried out without added stress or heartache.

Estate Taxes

Ah, taxes—the one topic that can clear out a party faster than a poorly timed joke about the host's cooking. But stick with me here because understanding estate taxes is crucial for minimizing financial burdens on your partner and heirs. Estate taxes, or the tax that applies to the property transferred from a deceased person to their heirs, can be hefty, depending on the value of the estate and the laws in your area.

Here's where effective planning comes into play. Strategies like gifting assets while you're still alive, setting up trust funds, or even making sure your financial records are impeccable can significantly reduce the tax burden on your estate. This means more of your legacy goes to your loved ones than Uncle Sam. Consulting with a financial advisor who understands the nuances of estate taxes in mixed-orientation marriages can offer tailored advice that maximizes your estate's value and minimizes tax liabilities.

Legal Documents

Last but not least, let's talk about paperwork. Ensuring that all your legal documents are in order, such as power of attorney, living wills, and healthcare proxies, is like making sure you have the right gear before a hiking trip. These documents speak for you when you can't, ensuring that your wishes regarding medical decisions, asset management, and end-of-life care are clear.

Having these documents in place is particularly important in mixed-orientation marriages, where unsupportive family members might contest legal next-of-kin status. A power of attorney can designate your partner to manage your financial affairs if you cannot, while a healthcare proxy can ensure they have a say in medical decisions. It's about safeguarding your autonomy and ensuring your partner's legal standing is solid, regardless of the trail ahead.

So, while estate planning might not be the most exhilarating topic, it's undeniably one of the most important, especially in a mixed-orientation marriage. It's about crafting a plan that protects your partner, respects your wishes, and avoids leaving a legal tangle for your loved ones to unravel. With the right preparation, you can ensure that your legacy is a testament to your life and love, not a burden or a battleground.

Health Insurance and Benefits Challenges

When one partner in a mixed-orientation marriage comes out, it can sometimes feel like you're both starting a complicated dance where someone keeps changing the music. Navigating health insurance during such transitions is a classic example. It's like suddenly discovering a new rulebook, and nobody thought to give you a copy. Let's break down the steps so you can dance through this without stepping on too many toes.

Firstly, understanding your health insurance options and ensuring that both partners maintain continuous coverage can be like playing a game of musical chairs. The key here is to act quickly and knowledgeably. If you were previously covered under one partner's family policy, changes in your relationship status might affect this arrangement. Reviewing your current policy to see how coverage might change if your marital status does is crucial. For instance, some insurers may require that you remain legally married to maintain spousal coverage, while others might recognize domestic partnerships or civil unions. If one partner is coming out and it leads to a separation, you may need to look into individual health plans. Marketplaces established by the Affordable Care Act can be a good place to search for coverage that meets your needs without breaking the bank.

Now, let's talk about negotiating employee benefits. This is where the dance gets a bit more intricate. Employee benefits like dependent care, bereavement leave, and health insurance are often designed with traditional marriages in mind. However, many companies are becoming more inclusive. If your workplace hasn't yet caught up, it might be time to chat with your HR department. Approach this conversation armed with knowledge and a positive but firm attitude. Explain how inclusive benefits are not just good for employees but are also good for business, enhancing employee satisfaction and loyalty. Some employers may also offer access to legal services through employee assistance programs (EAPs), which can be helpful if you need specific advice.

Legal changes in marriage recognition can dramatically affect health and other benefits, making it essential to stay informed about the legal framework. For example, the legalization of same-sex marriage across the United States has significantly impacted benefits eligibility for countless couples. These changes mean employers must provide equal benefits for all legally married couples, regardless of sexual orientation. However, the specifics can vary by state, especially when laws are newly enacted or in flux. Keeping abreast of these changes is crucial. Resources like the Human Rights Campaign or local LGBTQ+ advocacy groups can provide up-to-date information on your rights and any recent legal shifts that might affect your benefits.

Advocating for fair coverage and equal benefits is like being the lead dancer in your health insurance tango. It's about taking proactive steps to ensure employers, insurance companies, and policymakers treat you and your partner fairly. This could mean writing letters, attending meetings, and joining advocacy groups pushing policy changes. Engaging in advocacy helps secure your rights and paves the way for greater equality for the LGBTQ+ community. Organizations such as Lambda Legal or the National Center for Lesbian Rights can offer guidance and support in these efforts, providing resources that help you advocate effectively.

Navigating the complexities of health insurance and employee benefits during significant life transitions is no small feat. It requires patience, perseverance, and a good dose of savvy negotiating. But with the right approach and resources, you can ensure that you and your partner are protected and supported, no matter how the music changes. This dance may be complex, but mastering the steps can lead to a sense of security and stability that makes all the effort worthwhile.

Prenuptial and Postnuptial Agreements

Let's pour a cup of coffee and chat about something that often gets brushed under the rug in the excitement of wedding bells or even during the recalibration of a marriage: prenuptial and postnuptial agreements. Think of these agreements as a relationship insurance policy—nobody plans for accidents, but boy, isn't it great to be prepared if one happens.

Purpose of Agreements

So, why consider a prenup or a postnup in a mixed-orientation marriage? Well, it's all about protecting both of you, ensuring that no matter how your relationship evolves, both partners feel secure and protected. These agreements can outline everything from how you'll handle finances, who gets the dog, or how you'll manage debt. It's not about mistrust; it's about mutual respect and preparedness. Think of it like setting the rules for a game before you start playing—it makes it more enjoyable knowing everyone's on the same page.

This preparation becomes even more critical in mixed-orientation marriages where the complexities of evolving identities and dynamics can introduce unique challenges. A well-crafted agreement can prevent potential conflicts, provide clarity and ensure that both partners' interests are safeguarded. Knowing you have a parachute when skydiving makes jumping out of the plane a little less daunting.

Drafting the Agreement

Drafting this agreement is like planning a road trip. You need to map out where you're going, decide on the stops, and figure out what to pack. In legal terms, this means being clear about what assets and debts each partner brings into the marriage and how you'd handle assets acquired during the marriage. Discussing spousal support might also be on the table, especially if there are significant disparities in earning potential or career sacrifices made by one partner.

The key here is fairness and foresight. It's about protecting assets and ensuring that both partners are supported, whatever the future holds. This could mean provisions for career development opportunities if one partner has put their career on hold or agreements on handling shared businesses. Transparency is your best friend in these discussions—the secret ingredient that makes these agreements stick.

Legal Guidance

Given the stakes, winging it with a DIY legal form from the internet is like trying to cut your hair before a big event—it might turn out okay, but if it doesn't, it will show. This is why you need a good attorney who understands the nuances of mixed-orientation marriages and can guide you through the legal thicket. They can help ensure that the agreement is comprehensive and enforceable. Different states have different rules about what can and can't be included in these agreements, and some require that each partner has legal counsel to ensure that there are no claims of unfair advantage.

An experienced attorney can provide invaluable advice on how to tailor the agreement to reflect your unique situation and ensure that it holds up in court, should it ever need to. They're like the expert guide on a wilderness expedition—sure, you could explore independently, but wouldn't you feel better with an expert leading the way?

Case Studies

Real-life examples can show how these agreements work. Consider the case of Bailey and Jamie. Bailey, a transgender man, married Jamie before his transition. They drafted a postnuptial agreement that outlined how they would handle medical expenses and changes in their financial situation due to Bailey's transition. This foresight proved invaluable in keeping both partners financially secure and the marriage strong during a challenging time.

Then there's the example of Sam and Bailey, a bisexual woman and a straight man who decided on a prenup before tying the knot. Their agreement included provisions for sharing the financial burden of Bailey's student loans, acquired before the marriage, and a plan for dividing investments they planned to make together. When they amicably parted ways years later, their prenup simplified what could have been a complicated and contentious divorce process.

These stories illustrate that while thinking about a prenup or postnup might not be the most romantic part of a relationship, it can be crucial in ensuring that all parties feel respected and protected, no matter what life throws your way.

Navigating the legal and financial aspects of a relationship, especially one as potentially complex as a mixed-orientation marriage, can be daunting. Yet, with the right preparation and understanding—securing your legal rights, planning your financial future, navigating potential separations, or setting clear terms through agreements—you set the stage for a relationship built on clarity and mutual respect. As we close this chapter and look ahead, remember that the strength of a marriage lies not just in the love shared but also in the care taken to protect and nurture that love through every season of life. Ready for the next chapter? Let's keep turning the pages together.

FIVE

Family Dynamics and Social Relationships

Imagine trying to explain the plot of a sci-fi movie to a four-year-old. You'd simplify it. Talk about the friendly aliens and the colorful spaceships, skipping the complex backstories and quantum physics. Now, apply that to discussing your mixed-orientation marriage with your children. It's about distilling complex adult emotions and social dynamics into something digestible and reassuring for young minds. This isn't just about having "the talk"; it's about opening a dialogue that's age-appropriate, honest, and, most importantly, filled with love.

Talking to Children About Mixed-Orientation Marriage

Age-Appropriate Discussions

When you're planning to discuss your mixed-orientation marriage with your kids, the first step is to tailor your conversation to their level of understanding. It's like customizing a recipe to suit someone's taste—you wouldn't add hot sauce to a toddler's meal. For young children, this might mean explaining that just like some people prefer chocolate and some prefer vanilla, sometimes adults love differently, too. It's simple: "Mom loves another mom, and Dad loves a dad, and that's okay because love is what matters."

As they age, you can gradually introduce more complex ideas, such as sexual orientation and gender identity, always framing these in the context of love, respect, and family values. It's like gradually adding more spices to a dish as their palates mature, allowing them to appreciate deeper flavors without overwhelming them. The key is to keep the conversation open and ongoing. Children's understanding and curiosity will evolve, and they'll have new questions as they encounter different ideas about family and relationships.

Emphasizing Love and Security

No matter the age, the core message to your kids should be about the unchanging nature of your love and the security they have in your family. It's reassuring them that the family's love is like the sky—always there, no matter the weather. It might sound like, "No matter who Mom or Dad loves, we love you just the same and always will. Our family might look different, but our love for you will always be the same."

This reassurance is the emotional equivalent of a safety blanket, giving them the security they need to process the information about your family dynamics without fear or uncertainty. It's about ensuring they understand that your love for them is unwavering and unconditional, not tied to the structure of your marriage or the orientation of your partners.

Handling Questions

Kids are naturally curious, and their questions can be insightful and brutally honest. Preparing to answer these questions sensitively and honestly is like rehearsing for an important presentation—you need to know your stuff and be ready for unexpected queries. When they ask, "Why does Daddy like men now?" a response might be, "People can feel different about who they love as they learn more about themselves, just like sometimes you might feel like playing with different toys as you grow up."

It's important to answer their questions at a level they can understand and to steer the conversation back to the fundamentals of love and respect. Encourage them to ask questions whenever they arise and be patient; sometimes, you might need to answer the same question multiple times as they try to understand the concept fully.

Support Resources for Children

Providing children with resources that help them understand and adapt to changes in family dynamics can be as crucial as giving them a good breakfast—it sets them up for success. Books are particularly great tools. Titles like "And Tango Makes Three" by Justin Richardson and Peter Parnell or "In Our Mothers' House" by Patricia Polacco offer stories of diverse families, which can normalize different family structures and open up space for conversation.

Additionally, counseling and support groups designed for children of LGBTQ+ families can be invaluable. These resources offer them a safe space to express their feelings and meet other kids navigating similar experiences. It's like finding their tribe, where they can share, learn, and support each other in a guided, supportive environment.

Tackling the topic of your mixed-orientation marriage with your kids doesn't have to be daunting. With thoughtful preparation, a focus on the unchanging nature of your love, and the right support resources, you can guide them through understanding your family's unique story. It's about building a narrative together, one that's grounded in love, respect, and openness, setting a foundation for a lifetime of understanding and acceptance. So, take a deep breath, gather your resources, and prepare for some of the most honest and rewarding conversations you might ever have with your little ones.

Managing Relationships with Extended Family

Have you ever tried explaining your latest, slightly unconventional hobby to a room full of traditional relatives? Have you taken up nighttime skydiving or cheese sculpting? Now imagine that hobby is your mixed-orientation marriage. The room might spin faster. Discussing your relationship's unique nature with extended family often requires a blend of tact, timing, and tenacity, much like launching into a detailed explanation of why you believe moon cheese could be the next big thing.

Initial Disclosure Techniques

Timing is everything, isn't it? As you wouldn't propose a toast during a heated debate at the dinner table, choosing the right moment to discuss your marriage's orientation dynamics with extended family is crucial. It's about finding a moment when the conversation can be more than background noise. Maybe it's a quiet afternoon during a family visit or a planned dinner where family discussions are commonplace. The setting matters, too. A private, comfortable environment, away from the chaos of a family event, often sets the stage for a more meaningful and focused conversation. Here, you're not just dropping a bomb and running for cover; you're inviting understanding and dialogue.

Prepare for this talk as you would for an important presentation. Outline your key points: how you wish to be understood, your hopes for their support, and what this means for the family dynamics. It's not about seeking approval but about seeking respect and understanding. Be clear about what your relationship entails and perhaps preempt some common questions or misconceptions they might have. This clarity can help steer the conversation from sensationalism to genuine understanding and support.

Dealing With Varied Reactions

Let's be honest: not every family member will react with open arms and warm cookies. Reactions can range from loving acceptance to confusion or even rejection. It's like tossing a mix of spices into a pot; you're still determining the flavor once it's done. For those who respond with love and support, cherish and nurture these relationships. They can be your allies and advocates within the broader family network.

For the skeptics and the outright rejectors, arm yourself with patience and a strategy. Sometimes, simply giving them time to process the information helps. People may need space to adjust their perceptions and expectations. If faced with negativity or misunderstanding, it helps to have prepared responses: gentle corrections of misconceptions, reaffirmations of what your relationship means to you, and why their support matters. Remember, you don't have to convert them into champions of the cause, but establishing mutual respect is vital.

Educating Family Members

Education can be a powerful tool in transforming skepticism into support. Consider sharing resources like books, articles, or documentaries that explain the nuances of LGBTQ+ experiences and mixed-orientation marriages. These resources can act as conversation starters or reference points for family members trying to understand your situation better. It's a bit like giving them a manual to the latest tech gadget—they might not know how to use it at first, but with the right instructions, they'll see how it fits into their world.

Sometimes, inviting them to open events or workshops on LGBTQ+ issues can also be helpful. These experiences can broaden their perspectives and give them a more profound understanding of the community. It's about showing them the bigger picture, where love and respect are universal languages.

Boundary Setting

Finally, setting boundaries is crucial. It's about protecting your peace and ensuring your relationship is respected. Communicate your limits: what kinds of comments are hurtful, what behaviors are unacceptable, and how you expect to be treated. It's okay to limit or end conversations that feel disrespectful or harmful. Setting these boundaries is not about building walls but about laying down guardrails that keep your relationships healthy and your emotional well-being intact.

Navigating the dynamics with extended family when you're in a mixed-orientation marriage is never just about changing their views but about fostering an environment where love, respect, and understanding can grow. Whether through careful timing, managing reactions with empathy, educating with resources, or setting clear boundaries, each step is about nurturing a family dynamic that supports and upholds the dignity of your unique relationship. As you proceed, keep your heart open but your boundaries firm, allowing space for growth, understanding, and, hopefully, acceptance.

The Role of Friendships: Losses and Gains

Imagine your social circle as a garden you've lovingly tended over the years, filled with various relationships like flowers in full bloom. Then, revealing your mixed-orientation marriage is like a season change—some friendships will thrive, others may wither, and you might even plant new seeds. This shift can be as refreshing as it is daunting, but understanding the dynamics of friendships during such transitions can turn these experiences into opportunities for growth and deeper connections.

Navigating changes in friendships often begins with an understanding that not all friendships are equipped to weather the storm of significant life changes. Just as some plants thrive in direct sunlight and others prefer the shade, different friendships serve different roles and capacities in our lives. When you share the evolution of your marriage, some friends might surprise you with their support, blossoming into stronger allies, while others might struggle, showing signs of discomfort or withdrawal. It's not uncommon for some to fall away, unable to understand or accept the changes. This loss, while painful, is often a natural part of life's ebb and flow—a pruning process that, although challenging, can lead to a healthier social ecosystem. It's crucial to approach this process with a spirit of acceptance, focusing on the quality of support rather than the quantity of your social connections.

On the brighter side, such transitions open space for new friendships, especially with individuals or groups who empathize with or share similar experiences in the mixed-orientation dynamic. These new connections often arise from places you might expect the least— support groups, online communities, or even chance encounters during events. These friends can be like rain after a long drought, bringing fresh perspectives and understanding, enriching your life in ways you hadn't anticipated. They often come equipped with an intrinsic understanding of your challenges, offering relevant and empathetic support. Embracing these new friendships can invigorate your social life and provide a robust support network that resonates more closely with your current realities.

The benefits of cultivating a supportive community of friends during this period cannot be overstated. Friends who respect and understand the dynamics of your marriage can be pillars of strength, offering shoulders to lean on when the going gets tough. They can mirror back the resilience and love that define your relationship, reinforcing the normalcy and validity of your family structure. This support is crucial for your well-being and for maintaining a healthy relationship with your partner. It provides a buffer against the societal pressures and prejudices that mixed-orientation couples often face, allowing you to navigate your relationship journey more confidently and with less isolation.

Rebuilding or expanding your social circles after coming out requires a proactive approach. Start by exploring new places and communities that fit your current situation. Whether attending LGBTQ+ events, joining forums, or participating in workshops focusing on diversity and inclusion, each step can be a building block toward a richer, more supportive social network. Don't shy away from introducing your partner to your new friends or involving them in community activities. This helps solidify your relationship and integrates your partner into a social framework that acknowledges and celebrates your union just as it is.

As you navigate the changes in your friendships, remember that each interaction, new connection, and even the loss of old ties is part of aligning your social circle with your true self. It's about nurturing relationships that bring out the best in you, challenge you to grow, and provide a safe space to be your true self. So, take heart, step out, and let your social garden evolve to reflect the beautiful diversity of your life and love.

Creating New Traditions in the Evolving Family Structure

Think of traditions as the glue that holds the pages of your family's storybook together. The recurring themes and rituals give your family its unique flavor—a blend of shared memories and collective values. In a mixed-orientation marriage, where family dynamics may shift and evolve, reimagining or introducing new traditions can be like updating your family's operating system to reflect better and celebrate this diversity. It's not about discarding the old but rather about expanding and enriching the family experience to include all its members authentically.

The importance of traditions in maintaining family cohesion cannot be overstated. They are the rhythms to which your family's heart beats, from the annual summer picnics to the bedtime stories passed down through generations. These rituals provide a sense of continuity, particularly comforting in times of change. When one or both parents come out, it can shake the foundations of a family's understood identity. Here, traditions stabilize forces, reaffirming the family's core values and reinforcing that while some things may change, the fundamental bonds of love and support remain unaltered.

Therefore, creating new traditions is an opportunity to reinforce these bonds and celebrate the family's inclusivity. For instance, you might start a family tradition of attending or participating in LGBTQ+ events, such as Pride parades or community arts projects. This brings the family together in a shared activity and publicly affirms your family's support for each other and the LGBTQ+ community. It's a powerful way of saying, "We are proud of who we are, and we stand together." Alternatively, you might introduce a weekly family night where members can share something about their week or choose an activity for everyone to enjoy. This tradition can become a platform for open communication, fostering a deeper understanding of each other's lives and an appreciation for each member's uniqueness.

The role of rituals in providing stability and a sense of normalcy is equally crucial. These small, often daily practices embed security and predictability into your family's routine. It might be as simple as having breakfast together every Sunday morning or as specific as reading from a particular collection of inspirational stories each night. These rituals act as anchors, holding the family steady in rough waters. They reassure children and adults that some things remain constant and the family unit persists even as individual identities and dynamics evolve.

To illustrate the impact of integrating new traditions, consider the case of the Martinez family. After Maria came out as bisexual, she and her husband, Carlos, were initially uncertain about how to address this with their children. They decided to introduce a new tradition called "Family Story Time," where each member, including the children, would share stories or experiences from their lives. This ritual helped the children understand their mother's identity in a safe and nurturing environment and encouraged them to express their thoughts and feelings. Over time, this tradition became a cherished part of their family life, enhancing their bond and providing a forum for ongoing dialogue about changes within the family.

In another example, the Chen family, with one transgender parent, started a new tradition of volunteering at a local LGBTQ+ youth center. This activity helped the children understand the broader context of their parent's transition and fostered a sense of pride and solidarity with the LGBTQ+ community. It also offered the parents new ways to connect with their children through a shared commitment to social justice and community support.

Embracing new traditions in your evolving family structure is not just about adaptation; it's about celebration. It's an affirmation that while life may lead you down unexpected paths, the journey can be rich with new rituals and customs that honor every member's identity. These traditions help shape your family's unique story, creating a colorful, inclusive, and dynamic picture of shared life and love. So, as you consider the traditions that resonate with your family's values and experiences, remember that each new ritual or practice you introduce is a building block in the beautiful structure of your family life, reinforcing the message that change can be a path to more profound unity and joy.

Dealing with Social Stigma and Isolation

Imagine walking into a party where you're pretty sure you stick out like a sore thumb, not because of what you're wearing, but because of who you love. That's a day in the life when you're in a mixed-orientation marriage—a scenario where whispers might be a bit louder and stares a touch longer. Understanding the origins and forms of social stigma associated with such unions is like understanding why certain music genres don't play well in every crowd. It stems from long-standing societal norms, a cocktail of historical biases, and a lack of understanding that brews misconceptions and prejudice. This stigma can seep into various facets of life, affecting everything from family gatherings to professional interactions, casting a shadow over the everyday lives of those involved.

Dealing with this stigma isn't about changing the music to suit the crowd but about wearing your unique playlist with pride and maybe, just maybe, teaching others to appreciate a new tune. Strengthening your internal family support is foundational. It's the VIP backstage pass that keeps you rooted. This means ensuring that every family member is on the same page, understands the challenges, and is ready to offer emotional support or stand up against discriminatory remarks. It's about creating a home environment where open conversations about feelings and experiences are as normal as Sunday breakfast. Sometimes, this might also involve seeking external counseling to fortify your emotional resilience. Counselors or therapists specializing in LGBTQ+ issues can provide tools and strategies to manage the stress and negativity that stigma can bring into your lives, much like a sound engineer ensuring every microphone is perfectly tuned before a big performance.

But what about when you step out of your safe space? Reducing isolation by connecting with similar families can be as refreshing as finding fans of your favorite obscure band. This connection can happen in support groups, community centers, or online platforms where people share similar experiences. These spaces offer solace and practical advice on navigating the complexities of a mixed-orientation marriage. They remind you that you're not alone, that others are dancing to a similar beat, and together, you can turn the volume up on awareness and acceptance.

And speaking of increasing the volume, participating in public education efforts is crucial in changing the broader societal playlist. It's about taking the stage and sharing your story, whether speaking at events, participating in documentaries, or writing articles. All sharing is an opportunity to dispel myths and humanize your experiences. It's about showing that at the core of every mixed-orientation marriage is love, commitment, and the same daily negotiations that mark any relationship. These public engagements are not just about seeking acceptance but about educating society to foster a more inclusive community that values diversity in all its forms.

Navigating the world while in a mixed-orientation marriage does indeed come with its set of challenges, from dealing with whispers and stares to battling outright discrimination. Yet, through strengthening your internal support, connecting with others on similar paths, and engaging in public education, you can forge a path of resilience and advocacy. It's about wearing your unique playlist proudly, dancing to your rhythm, and perhaps inspiring others to appreciate the richness of diverse melodies in the symphony of human relationships. So, keep your head high, your support network strong, and your voice louder, for every step you take in authenticity and openness paves the way for a more understanding and inclusive world. In this journey of breaking stereotypes and building bridges, remember every conversation, every shared story, and every connection is a note in the harmonious melody of progress.

Finding and Building Community Support

Imagine planting a garden where each plant represents a different community support system. Some plants are local, thriving on direct sunlight, while others flourish in the digital realm, needing just a bit of Wi-Fi to grow. Cultivating a support network in a mixed-orientation marriage is like gardening. You need a variety of supports that can thrive in different environments and conditions, providing you with a resilient, flourishing support system that can weather any season.

Identifying Supportive Communities

Finding communities that resonate with the unique experiences of mixed-orientation marriages can sometimes feel like searching for a needle in a haystack. Start local. Look for LGBTQ+ community centers, which often offer resources and social groups that understand the nuances of your situation. Many cities have groups for mixed-orientation couples, offering a space to share experiences and advice. If you're unsure where to start, a quick online search or visiting your city's community health centers can point you in the right direction.

Libraries and bookstores can also be unexpected goldmines for finding community connections. Look for books, flyers, or bulletin boards advertising local meet-ups or events. Attending LGBTQ+ friendly religious or spiritual services can connect you with a more supportive community. These venues offer spiritual support and connect you with a broader community that may share similar values and experiences.

Online and Virtual Support

In today's digital age, virtual communities are as vital as local ones, especially if you live in an area with less physical presence of supportive groups. Online forums, social media groups, and virtual meet-ups can provide invaluable support. Platforms like Reddit, Facebook, and even specific apps for LGBTQ+ individuals can offer anonymous and supportive spaces to discuss your experiences and challenges. These platforms allow you to connect with people across the globe who are navigating similar paths, providing perspectives and support that might not be available locally.

Moreover, many organizations host webinars, online workshops, and even virtual coffee meets to help you feel connected without leaving home. These resources are particularly valuable for those who live in areas where LGBTQ+ support is not readily accessible. They allow you to cultivate a garden of support that spans the globe, ensuring you have access to advice and friendship no matter where you are.

Creating Your Support Network

Sometimes, you might find that the specific support you're looking for doesn't exist yet in your area. When that happens, why not start your own group? Creating a local support network or group can seem daunting, but it's like planting a seed that could grow into a supportive tree for many. Begin by contacting local community centers or LGBTQ+ organizations to gauge interest. They often can provide space and initial support to get your group off the ground.

When organizing meetings, consider privacy and inclusivity. Make sure the meeting spots are safe and accessible for everyone. Setting an agenda can help keep discussions on track and ensure that all members feel they have a chance to share and participate. Establishing ground rules that respect confidentiality and promote a supportive environment is vital. This helps maintain privacy and creates a space where all members feel secure and valued.

Leveraging Community Resources

Don't forget about the larger community resources that can strengthen your support network. Many LGBTQ+ organizations offer social support, legal advice, counseling, and educational resources. Using these can give you the tools and knowledge to handle the challenges of a mixed-orientation marriage better.

Additionally, participating in community events, whether Pride parades, LGBTQ+ art shows, or public forums, can increase your visibility and the visibility of mixed-orientation marriages within the broader community. This helps reduce stigma and builds a network of allies who can offer support in unexpected ways.

As you put down roots in these various supportive communities, remember that each connection, each conversation, and each meeting enriches your support network, providing you with the strength and resilience to thrive in your marriage. Whether through local groups, online forums, or your initiatives, building a diverse and robust community support system is a dynamic and ongoing process that adapts to your growing needs and blossoms with your relationship. So, keep nurturing your garden of support, for it promises a harvest of friendship, understanding, and collective strength that can make all the difference in your journey.

As we wrap up this exploration into the world of community support, remember that every seed of effort you plant in building these connections has the potential to grow into something profoundly impactful. Not just for you but for others in similar situations, for your family, and for the broader community. You are cultivating support and enhancing the ecosystem of understanding and acceptance around mixed-orientation marriages. With this foundation, we turn our attention to the next chapter, where we explore the personal and collective journeys of growth and acceptance, further enriching our understanding and appreciation of the diverse paths that relationships can take.

Success Stories and Case Studies

Imagine your relationship as a complex dance routine, where every step, turn, and lift represents a form of communication. Now, picture that you and your partner are learning this dance in the middle of a bustling party—surrounded by distractions, different music playing on each speaker, and now and then, someone bumps into you, throwing off your rhythm. Communication in a mixed-orientation marriage can feel like a beautiful dance that requires understanding, patience, and much practice. Let's dive into a story that embodies the triumphs of such a dance.

Triumphs in Communication: A Couple's Journey

Developing Open Communication

Meet Bailey and Jordan, a couple waltzing through the complexities of a mixed-orientation marriage. Bailey identifies as bisexual, and Jordan as heterosexual. Early in their marriage, their communication resembled more of a chaotic foot-tapping than a synchronized waltz. Misunderstandings were frequent, and discussions about emotions or attractions were like stepping on each other's toes rather than moving in harmony.

The turning point came when they decided to treat communication as a skill they could learn and improve rather than a problem they couldn't solve. They began scheduling weekly 'dance lessons'—dedicated times to talk openly about their feelings, fears, and desires without the distraction of daily chores or technology. These sessions weren't always easy. There were moments of discomfort and vulnerability, but each conversation helped them understand each other's rhythms better.

One technique they found particularly helpful was the 'emotional echo,' where they would repeat what the other said before responding. This simple act of mirroring helped ensure they weren't just hearing but understanding each other's steps, gradually smoothing their conversational dance into something more fluid and less fraught with missteps.

Overcoming Communication Barriers

A significant challenge they faced was discussing Bailey's attraction to other genders without Jordan feeling insecure or threatened. During one particularly tense discussion, Bailey used a metaphor of admiring a painting in a museum—an appreciation of beauty without the desire to take it home. This analogy struck a chord with Jordan, helping shift his perspective from insecurity to understanding.

They also introduced 'pause and reflect' timeouts in their discussions, a technique suggested by their communication coach. Whenever conversations became too intense or emotional, they would take a brief break to collect their thoughts and calm their emotions, preventing many potential arguments from escalating.

Role of Professional Help

Realizing they needed external guidance to fine-tune their communication skills, Bailey and Jordan started working with a communication coach specializing in LGBTQ+ relationships. This coach helped them develop personalized communication exercises and provided a neutral ground where they could practice and refine their techniques. The coach also introduced them to 'communication choreography,' where they learned to anticipate and respond to each other's emotional needs proactively.

Takeaways for Readers

Bailey and Jordan's journey offers valuable lessons. First, communication is viewed as a skill requiring ongoing attention and refinement, like maintaining form and poise in dance. Regular, dedicated discussions can transform your communicative missteps into a graceful ballet of understanding and empathy.

Second, metaphors and analogies should be used to bridge understanding gaps. Finding common or relatable ground through imagery can make a confusing conversation enlightening. Lastly, don't shy away from professional help. Like a dance instructor can refine your physical movements, a communication coach can fine-tune your conversational rhythms, turning discord into harmony.

Bailey and Jordan's story is a testament to the power of effective communication in navigating the intricate dance of a mixed-orientation marriage. Their journey from clumsy steps to a harmonious routine illustrates that with patience, practice, and a little professional guidance, couples can create a dialogue that survives and thrives amid the complexities of their unique relationship dynamics. So, take a leaf from their book, and may your communicative dance be just as enriching and successful.

Resilience in the Face of Adversity: One Family's Story

Imagine for a moment, you're in a boat caught in a storm, waves crashing all around—this is often what facing societal challenges feels like in a mixed-orientation marriage. Meet Linda and Mark, a couple whose journey through Linda's coming out as lesbian was anything but smooth sailing. Their story is not just about facing these tumultuous waves but learning to navigate them with grace and resilience. The external pressures were intense: stigmatization from their community, whispered judgments at PTA meetings, and the cold shoulder from friends they once considered close. These waves threatened to capsize their family boat, but Linda, Mark, and their two children learned to steer through these rough waters together.

Their secret? Open decks and clear skies—metaphorically speaking. Linda and Mark made it their mission to keep communication channels open between themselves and their children. They tackled the stigma head-on by initiating honest discussions at home about their challenges. This openness transformed their home into a sanctuary where each family member could voice fears or frustrations without judgment, turning their family dynamics into the lifeline that kept them afloat. They adopted a family motto, "Us against the problem, not us against each other," which became their anchor in every storm. This approach didn't change the external noises—those were and are still there—but fortified their home, allowing them to support each other through external adversities.

Their resilience was further tested when Mark lost his job due to a company's discomfort with his wife's orientation—a blow that could have shattered their stability. However, it pulled them closer instead of letting this challenge divide them. They rallied as a family, discussing financial adjustments transparently and supporting Mark in his job search, turning a period of potential despair into collective problem-solving and mutual support.

Community Support

Finding and building a supportive community was crucial in bolstering their resilience. Initially isolated, they reached out to online forums and local support groups for mixed-orientation marriages. These platforms provided emotional support and practical advice on navigating the complexities of their situation. Attending community events and LGBTQ+ gatherings also connected them with families riding the same stormy seas, which was incredibly validating. Here, Linda met Emma, a counselor specializing in LGBTQ+ family dynamics, who introduced them to resilience-building techniques that became their compass in navigating these challenges.

These community connections did more than offer sympathy—they provided a mirror reflecting that their struggles were part of a larger narrative, one that many other families were also living. This realization was a powerful antidote to their isolation, reinforcing that they were not alone in their journey. The community became their harbor, a place to dock their family boat safely amid the storm, to rest, repair, and prepare for the next wave.

Resilience Techniques

Emma introduced them to several resilience-building techniques they integrated into their family life. One such technique was the "Weekly Family Check-In"—a dedicated weekly time where each family member shared their highs and lows. This ritual became a cornerstone of their resilience, ensuring ongoing communication and preemptive support for any member feeling the weight of external pressures.

Another technique was "Role-Reversal Role-Play," in which family members occasionally switched roles during discussions to see perspectives from different angles. This exercise fostered empathy within the family and equipped them with the emotional insight to handle external misunderstandings more effectively. It was like rehearsing a play where everyone knew their lines and everyone else's, too, creating a cohesive family unit that could perform seamlessly in the face of societal challenges.

From Linda and Mark's story, we can extract some critical lessons. Building resilience in the face of adversity often requires turning inward to your family and outward to your community. It's about fortifying your internal dynamics with open communication and empathy while anchoring yourself in a supportive community that can provide external strength and validation. These strategies do not eliminate the challenges but empower you to meet them with a united front, turning your family's boat into a ship capable of navigating even the stormiest seas. So, as you face your waves, remember the power of open decks (communication), clear skies (transparency), and a good compass (community support), and you might just find that you can weather any storm together.

Navigating New Relationships Post-Divorce

Let's turn the page and meet Chris, a vibrant soul who found himself redefining his path after his mixed-orientation marriage came to a respectful close. Chris, who identifies as gay, was married to Anna, a wonderful woman and a steadfast ally. When they parted ways, it was less about a loss of love and more about gaining a proper understanding of themselves and each other. Stepping back into the dating scene, Chris carried a suitcase packed with lessons from his marriage, not just about love but about deeper self-awareness and mutual respect.

Starting anew is like hitting the reset button, but it's more like playing a new song on the guitar; the chords are familiar, but the rhythm is new. Chris approached dating with a mindset shaped profoundly by his past experiences. From day one, he knew the importance of transparency—there was no room for ambiguity about his identity or past journey. This open-book approach wasn't just about being honest with others and respecting his journey and the person he had become. Navigating through new interactions, Chris found that his honesty acted like a magnet, attracting individuals who admired his authenticity and shared similar values of openness and integrity.

However, re-entering the dating pool was not without its ripples. The challenge often lay in the assumptions people made about his past marriage. Some dates turned cautious, almost clinical, fearing Chris was still on the fence about his orientation. To navigate these waters, Chris learned the art of storytelling—sharing his narrative not as a tale of confusion but as a saga of self-discovery and respect for his and Anna's journeys. He framed his past not as a period of doubt but as a chapter of growth that led him to become more in tune with his authentic self. This narrative shift helped clear misunderstandings and allowed his dates to see the strength and clarity he had gained from his marriage.

Success in his new relationships didn't come from swiping right on the perfect profile but building connections based on shared understanding and emotional depth. One particular relationship with Michael, a teacher passionate about art and advocacy, blossomed beautifully. Their bond was strengthened by their mutual commitment to communication and honesty, echoed in their nightly conversations that shifted between earnest, deep discussions and bursts of laughter over cups of warm tea.

For those fluttering on the edges of re-entering the dating world after a similar chapter, here's a nugget of advice from Chris's tale: Embrace your story with pride. Your past experiences, including a mixed-orientation marriage, are not just footnotes in your life; they are chapters that contribute to the narrative complexity of who you are. When stepping into new relationships, carry forward the lessons of open communication and self-respect. Let these guide you in establishing connections rooted in understanding and authenticity.

Navigating new relationships after the end of a marriage is like setting sail on a voyage where the compass is your learned experiences, and the horizon is filled with possibilities. Embrace the journey with openness, learn from the waves, and sail toward connections that resonate with the deepest parts of your being. Remember, every interaction is a step toward discovering another heart and rediscovering your own in reflecting on new experiences. So, set your sails, and let the winds of honest conversations and heartfelt connections guide you to the shores of new beginnings.

Long-Term Success: Staying Together Against the Odds

Picture this: two trees planted side by side, growing intertwined over the years, weathering storms, and thriving despite the odds. This is the story of Sarah and Mike, a couple whose marriage could have been written off by any betting man early on due to the revelation of Sarah's lesbian identity after a decade of marriage. Yet, here they are, two decades later, not just surviving but flourishing together. Their tale isn't just about sticking it out; it's a testament to the power of adapting, sharing, and deeply committing to one another through a dynamic and evolving relationship.

Sarah and Mike's journey of sustaining love and commitment began with a foundation of deep friendship and mutual respect, which they had cultivated since college. When Sarah came out, the ground beneath them could have easily crumbled. However, their intrinsic friendship provided a sturdy base from which they could renegotiate their relationship. They approached these changes with a willingness to be flexible and to redefine what their marriage looked like. This adaptability became their superpower, allowing them to maintain a core connection despite changes in the romantic and sexual dynamics of their relationship. They shifted toward an understanding that their marriage could include co-parenting their children, managing their household together, and supporting each other's journeys of self-discovery and romantic pursuits outside the marriage.

Adapting to changes was more than just big, sweeping gestures or decisions. It was in the daily nuances—choosing to communicate openly about feelings, attractions, and needs without judgment or insecurity. Mike, for instance, learned to express his initial feelings of insecurity without framing them as accusations. At the same time, Sarah provided reassurance of her commitment and love, affirming that her orientation did not diminish her affection and dedication to their family. This ongoing dialogue helped them navigate the complex emotions that naturally surfaced, turning potential stumbling blocks into stepping stones for deeper understanding and connection.

The glue that held Sarah and Mike together was their shared values and goals. From the outset, they were aligned on key aspects of their lives—raising their children in a nurturing environment, supporting each other's careers, and maintaining a home filled with laughter and openness. These shared goals acted as a compass, guiding them through turbulent times. Even as they navigated the complexities of a mixed-orientation marriage, their shared visions for their family and mutual respect and happiness allowed them to continuously recalibrate and realign their paths. It was never about sacrificing one's happiness for the other but finding harmony where both could thrive.

Let Mike and Sarah's story inspire those reading this and make them wonder how to fortify their relationships against the odds. Embrace flexibility in how you view and structure your relationship. It's okay to deviate from traditional scripts. Love, after all, isn't a one-size-fits-all. Cultivate a garden of shared values and goals, and let them be your guide when the winds of change blow. Most importantly, keep the lines of communication open. Talk about everything—the good, the bad, and the confusing. You'll find your strength and resilience through these conversations as a couple.

Their story underscores a profound truth: the heart of long-term success in any marriage, mixed-orientation or otherwise, lies in the continual commitment to grow together and support each other unconditionally. It's not the absence of challenges that strengthens a marriage but how these challenges are met—with openness, understanding, and a willingness to adapt. So take a leaf from their book: let your relationship evolve, ensure it's anchored in shared dreams and values, and talk, always talk. In this dance of life, let your steps be guided by love and resilience, and like Sarah and Mike, you may just find yourself looking back over decades not just of challenges overcome but of a life richly shared and profoundly cherished.

Lessons Learned from Failed Marriages

Imagine you're piecing together a jigsaw puzzle, one that forms a picture of your life and marriage. Sometimes, despite every effort, a piece just doesn't fit, no matter how much you want it to. This is often the case in some mixed-orientation marriages, where despite love and best intentions, the pieces might come together differently. Let's explore some lessons gleaned from those who've walked through the dissolution of their marriages, not with a sense of failure, but with profound insights and unexpected gains.

The dissolution of a marriage, especially a mixed-orientation one, can be likened to a garden that, despite careful tending, doesn't thrive in the expected ways. Some plants might wither in these gardens, but this clearing can give space for new growth, and sometimes, even more resilient plants emerge. For instance, consider Jamie and Taylor's story. Married for several years with two kids, Jamie came out as transgender. Despite efforts to recalibrate their marriage, they realized their paths had diverged too significantly. Reflecting on their experience, they noted several pitfalls that could help others in similar situations. Communication, while open, often missed the emotional depth and acknowledgment of each other's profound identity shifts. They learned too late in their marriage the importance of truly understanding and empathizing with each other's journeys beyond just the surface adjustments.

Their insights highlight a common issue: fully understanding each other's personal growth. To avoid this, it's essential to communicate and connect with each other's emotions, making sure both partners feel genuinely seen and understood. It's more than just sharing updates; it's about sharing your inner thoughts and feelings.

From the ashes of their marriage's end, Jamie and Taylor found paths leading to personal fulfillment and better alignment with their identities. Taylor dove into advocacy work for LGBTQ+ rights, channeling her experiences into helping others, while Jamie found love that resonated with his true self. Their story underscores that sometimes, the end of a marriage isn't just an end; it's a doorway to new beginnings that can be more aligned with each individual's truth and happiness. This highlights how endings, often draped in the garb of failure, can be set up for future successes, where personal growth and fulfillment take center stage.

Recognizing when to let go of a relationship that isn't sustainable is like knowing when to seek shelter from a storm that won't clear. It involves understanding the signs of fundamental mismatches in needs and visions for the future that no effort can reconcile. Here, guidance comes from acknowledging persistent feelings of fulfillment or authenticity in the relationship. Are both partners growing, or is the relationship stifling? It involves honest self-reflection and, often, challenging conversations that might conclude with recognizing that separation could be the healthiest choice. Moving forward then consists of doing so with respect, care, and a commitment to managing the dissolution constructively, focusing on healing and growth rather than blame and bitterness.

Stories like Jamie and Taylor's remind us of the complexities of marriage, especially in mixed-orientation relationships. They show us that while not all marriages last, each teaches valuable lessons. These lessons about connection, understanding, personal growth, and sometimes letting go can enrich future relationships, whether romantic, familial, or with oneself. As we navigate these relationships, let's keep open hearts and minds ready to learn from each experience and embrace new beginnings. Every ending holds the potential for new stories to unfold.

Cultural Variations in Mixed-Orientation Marriages

Navigating a mixed-orientation marriage is like blending spices from different corners of the globe; each mix produces a distinct flavor, and every culture adds its unique twist. Globally, the perception and handling of mixed-orientation marriages vary widely, shaped by cultural norms, legal frameworks, and societal acceptance. Let's expand our understanding by exploring how different cultures handle these marriages, celebrating the diversity of experiences and the universal challenges they share.

In many Western societies, acceptance of mixed-orientation marriages has grown, especially with the increasing recognition of LGBTQ+ rights. However, in more traditional societies, these marriages often have to deal with a complex mix of cultural expectations and family obligations. Take, for instance, a couple from India, where arranged marriages are still prevalent, and LGBTQ+ rights are only beginning to catch the public's eye. Here, the revelation of a spouse's LGBTQ+ identity could disrupt not just their marriage but the extended family's standing in their community. The couple might face immense pressure to maintain a facade of a conventional marriage to uphold family honor, often at the cost of their mental health and happiness.

Despite the challenges, there are stories of resilience and adaptation. For example, Aarav and Meera, a mixed-orientation couple from Delhi, turned their marriage into a strong friendship and focused on raising their children in a nurturing environment. They found support through online communities and discreet support groups, where they could share experiences and get advice without fearing societal backlash. This allowed them to fulfill their family responsibilities and provided a network of understanding and support, showing how couples in restrictive environments navigate their complex situations.

Shifting our gaze to South America, where machismo culture prevails, the challenges faced by mixed-orientation marriages take on different shades. In Brazil, for example, the vibrant LGBTQ+ community in urban areas like São Paulo contrasts sharply with conservative rural areas where traditional gender roles are deeply entrenched. Carlos and Juliana, living in a small Brazilian town, had to balance their truths with the expectations of their tight-knit community. They did so by participating in local community events and gradually introducing LGBTQ+ advocacy, fostering gradual changes in perception within their community. Their journey underscores the importance of patience and gradual influence in challenging deep-seated cultural norms, showing that change is possible, even in the most traditional settings.

Cultural Resources and Support

Exploring the resources and support systems available to mixed-orientation marriages across different cultures, we find a spectrum of availability and effectiveness. In many Western countries, there are extensive legal protections and a plethora of resources ranging from counseling services to support groups dedicated to LGBTQ+ rights.

These resources provide couples the tools to navigate their relationships openly and safely.

However, such resources might be limited or non-existent in more conservative parts of the world. In these areas, the internet becomes a lifeline. Online forums and international NGOs often serve as the only source of support for mixed-orientation couples. They provide anonymity and a global community of people facing similar challenges, offering advice, comfort, and, sometimes, a plan to seek asylum in more accepting countries.

One inspiring example comes from a virtual support group initiated by a woman in Kenya, where LGBTQ+ rights are severely restricted. This group started as a small WhatsApp chat and grew into a robust online community, offering everything from legal advice to psychological support. It became a source of hope for many couples in similar situations across Africa, showing how digital platforms can overcome geographical and cultural barriers to provide support and advocacy.

These stories from around the world highlight the diverse ways in which mixed-orientation marriages are navigated and supported across different cultural contexts. They underscore the universal challenges of acceptance and identity within these relationships and illustrate the resilience and creativity with which couples maintain their bonds, navigate societal expectations, and seek out support communities. From leveraging online platforms in conservative societies to engaging in community advocacy in more liberal regions, these couples reflect a spectrum of strategies that underscore a common pursuit of love, understanding, and acceptance.

As we wrap up this chapter on mixed-orientation marriages worldwide, we see that while the challenges are similar, the ways to handle them are as varied as the cultures themselves. We move forward, inspired by the resilience and creativity of couples everywhere, ready to dive into the next part of our exploration of the complexities and successes of mixed-orientation marriages.

SEVEN

Dating and New Relationships

Stepping back into the dating world after a mixed-orientation marriage can feel like jumping into a pool after a long winter. It's refreshing and shocking, and you're unsure whether to dive headfirst or ease in one toe at a time. But here you are, swim cap in hand (okay, maybe not literally), ready to swim in new waters. This chapter is your poolside buddy, ready to hand you a towel, offer a high-five, and remind you that the water's fine. Let's explore the nuances of dating as a LGBTQ+ individual post-marriage—no armbands needed, promise.

Entering the Dating World: Tips for LGBTQ+ Individuals

Embrace Your Identity

First things first: embracing your identity. Imagine that each aspect of your identity is a unique instrument in the grand orchestra, and that is you. Being open and confident about who you are is like owning the melody you play. It's not just about being loud; it's about being proud, even if your tune differs from the others. Embracing your identity in the dating world is crucial. It's the key that unlocks genuine connections. If you're upfront about who you are, you'll likely find someone who appreciates your true self, not just the version you think they want to see. This authenticity resonates deeply in LGBTQ+ dating, where understanding and respecting diverse identities can significantly enrich relationships. So, tune your instrument, play your melody proudly, and remember, the right audience will love your concert.

Finding the Right Venues

Next up is finding suitable venues. This isn't just about the physical spaces that are LGBTQ+ friendly, though these are important. It's also about choosing platforms where you feel safe and supported. Think of it like selecting the right gym. Some folks prefer the all-inclusive places with pools and juice bars, while others thrive in a small, niche studio that offers specialized classes. In the dating world, this could mean anything from LGBTQ+ bars and clubs to online dating sites and apps that cater specifically to LGBTQ+ people. The key here is comfort and safety. You want a venue where you can strut your stuff without worry, knowing that the environment aligns with your vibe and values.

Navigating LGBTQ+ Dating Dynamics

Navigating the dynamics of LGBTQ+ dating can sometimes feel like learning a new dance. Each community has its rhythms and steps. There might be unspoken rules about flirting, the pace of relationships, or how to communicate effectively. Misunderstandings can occur, especially if you're new to the scene or re-entering the dating world after a long hiatus. It's like you're stepping onto a dance floor where everyone else seems to know the steps. Don't worry about a misstep or two! The key is to keep dancing, to learn from each interaction, and not to be afraid to ask for guidance. Most communities are more than willing to embrace someone sincere about learning and respecting their norms.

Support Networks

Finally, lean on support networks. These are your cheerleaders, your coaches, and sometimes, your lifeguards. LGBTQ+ support networks can offer everything from dating advice to emotional support. They can help you navigate the complexities of LGBTQ+ dating with a wealth of resources at your fingertips. These networks can be found in LGBTQ+ centers, online forums, and informal social groups. Engaging with these communities helps you feel connected and broadens your understanding of the diverse experiences within the LGBTQ+ spectrum. It's like having a team behind you, one that cheers you on when you score a date and offers you a pep talk when things don't go as planned.

Returning to the dating pool, remember that each swim strengthens you. Embrace your identity, choose your venues wisely, learn the dance of LGBTQ+ dating dynamics, and don't hesitate to rely on your support networks. With each stroke, you'll not only get better at navigating these waters, but you'll also enjoy the swim a whole lot more. So, goggles on—let's make a splash!

Dating After Coming Out: Advice for Heterosexual Partners

Imagine you've been playing a particular role in a long-running theater production, and suddenly, you're cast in a completely new play with a different script. This shift might feel daunting, and the thought of stepping onto a new stage can stir up a mix of excitement and nerves. That's like re-entering the dating scene after your spouse has come out. It's a whole new act, one where your previous role as a partner in a mixed-orientation marriage has given you unique insights and perhaps some reservations about opening your heart again.

Adjusting Expectations

First off, let's talk about adjusting expectations. If your previous relationship unfolded unexpectedly (like discovering new aspects of your partner's identity), you might be carrying a script that anticipates surprises or hidden truths. It's natural to feel cautious, but here's the kicker: every dating experience is a fresh scene, and carrying over too many assumptions from the last can throw you off your game. Think of it this way: you wouldn't wear a heavy winter coat just because it once snowed in April, right? Similarly, allow each new encounter to stand on its own. This doesn't mean throwing caution to the wind but rather allowing yourself to be open to the possibility that love can and does show up in unexpected and wonderful ways. Embrace the idea that just as you've grown and evolved, so too can your experiences and relationships.

Learning from Past Relationships

Reflecting on your previous marriage is like rewinding and replaying your favorite movie scenes to catch details you missed the first time. Dive into what your marriage taught you about your needs, desires, and deal-breakers. Were there moments you felt unheard or overcompromising? These reflections aren't about dwelling on the past but understanding your relationship dynamics more deeply. This insight is invaluable; it's like having a roadmap highlighting which roads you'd like to explore and which to bypass. Carry forward the lessons learned, but leave behind any baggage that might weigh down your future explorations. Remember, every relationship teaches us something valuable, even if it's knowing what we don't want.

Dating as a Single Parent

If you're juggling the roles of single parent and eager dater, integrating these aspects of your life can seem as tricky as a circus balancing act. Here's the secret: keep the communication lines open. Be upfront about your parenting commitments because, let's face it, your kids are part of the package deal. Involving someone new in your life isn't just about finding a match for you and a fit for your family dynamic. Schedule dates when you have parenting downtime or involve your kids in casual group activities to observe interactions. It's about finding a balance that respects your need for personal connection and your responsibilities as a parent. Think of it as choreographing a dance with your kids in the audience; you want them to enjoy the music, too.

Rebuilding Self-Esteem

Now, about polishing your self-esteem, which might have taken a hit after your spouse came out. It's time to dust off those doubts. Begin by affirming your worth daily. Self-esteem is like a muscle; the more you exercise it with positive affirmations and self-compassion, the stronger it becomes. Dive into activities that make you feel good about yourself, whether a hobby, exercise or spending time with friends who lift you. Remember, you are not defined by your past relationship but by the many qualities that make you uniquely you. Dating again is as much about rediscovering yourself as meeting someone new. So, step out with the confidence of someone who knows their worth and is ready to explore the possibilities of new connections.

As you navigate these new waters, keep your head high and your heart open. Adjusting your expectations, learning from your past, managing dating alongside parenting, and rebuilding your self-esteem are all part of the script for this new act in your life. Embrace it with enthusiasm and the wisdom of your experiences, and who knows? The next great love story might just be yours.

Online Dating: Safety and Setting Expectations

Venturing into online dating can often feel like you're trying to order a meal from a 15-page menu—overwhelming, with too many options and just a bit exciting. The key to navigating the vast digital world is finding the right platform that fits your personal and safety needs. Think of each dating platform as a different restaurant in a huge food court; some offer quick snacks (casual dating), others serve gourmet meals (serious relationships), and some are proud of their organic ingredients (niche interests). Choosing the right platform means checking the menu (the platform's features) and reviews (user feedback) to ensure it satisfies your specific dietary (dating) needs. Safety features, like food safety ratings on restaurant windows, are a must. Look for apps that give you control over who sees your profile and how you interact with others. Privacy settings, reporting mechanisms, and user verification are the salt, pepper, and napkin—essential for a clean and safe dining (dating) experience.

Creating a safe profile is like preparing a dish to present at a culinary competition; it must be appealing yet true to what's in it. The key ingredient here is honesty—letting your true self shine through without revealing too much personal information (like exactly where you get your spices). A good profile is like a well-seasoned dish; it gives enough flavor to entice interest and leaves them wanting more. Use pictures that show your personality and interests without exposing too much personal data. Descriptive language that speaks to who you are can act like a spice that perfectly complements a dish, making your profile memorable and genuine.

Setting realistic expectations is like not expecting a fast-food joint to serve five-star cuisine. Online dating is unpredictable, and while you might hope to meet 'The One' on your first try, it's more like sampling small bites at a tapas bar—you need to try a few before you find your favorite. Remember that not every interaction will lead to a deep connection, and that's okay. Approach each conversation as a chance to learn more about what does and doesn't suit your taste. Avoid common pitfalls like moving too fast or investing emotionally in a match before you've met them in person, which can lead to disappointment. Think of each chat as an ingredient in your dating recipe—some you'll love, some you'll pass on next time.

Finally, let's discuss safety protocols because nothing ruins a meal faster than a health hazard. In dating, this means protecting yourself from potential risks when transitioning from chatting online to meeting in person. Always meet in public spaces, like choosing a popular restaurant over a shady diner down an alley. Inform a friend about your plans, like leaving a recipe if someone else needs to cook the meal. Be attentive to red flags, such as requests for money or invasive questions—signs of a spoiled dish that must be returned. Trust your instincts; if something feels off, it's okay to cancel the order and leave the table.

Navigating online dating safely and effectively requires a mix of the right platform, an authentic and cautious profile presentation, realistic expectations, and stringent safety protocols. It's about finding the right blend of ingredients to create a dating experience that's enjoyable, safe, and ultimately satisfying. So, tie on your apron, fire up your profile, and get ready to mix, mingle, and maybe even find that perfect blend of flavors that suits your palate just right.

First Dates: Tips for Navigating New Relationships

Planning your first date after a significant relationship can feel like deciding what to cook for a dinner party when you must figure out the guests' tastes. You want to impress but also ensure everyone is comfortable and enjoys themselves. Here's a tip from the dating chef's secret cookbook: simplicity is key. Opt for a setting that encourages conversation and eases those first-date jitters. Think of places like a cozy café with a relaxed vibe, a picturesque park where you can stroll and talk, or a fun mini-golf course that adds a bit of playful competition to the mix. The goal here is to find a neutral, public space that feels safe and has the potential for a relaxed and enjoyable interaction. It's less about dazzling with extravagance and more about crafting an environment where you can be yourself.

Consider activities that help break the ice and prompt dialogue. There could be an art exhibit that could stir discussion or a food market that offers tastes worldwide, turning the date into a mini adventure. The idea is to engage in something that feels comfortable but leaves room for those spontaneous moments to help both of you drop your guards a bit. Consider it setting the stage for a play where the script is written in real time, guided by your mutual interests and interactions.

Moving on to communication tips, think of your words and expressions on this first date as the opening lines of your favorite book—you want them to be honest, engaging, and memorable. Openness and authenticity are essential; try to express your thoughts and feelings clearly and sincerely. It's like painting a picture of who you are, not with broad strokes trying to cover more canvas, but with detailed brushwork highlighting your true colors. However, while being open, remember to respect the pace of the newly forming relationship. It's a dance, not a race. Listen actively, showing genuine interest in the other person's words without pushing too hard or fast.

Managing expectations is also crucial. Enter the date with the mindset that this is an opportunity to learn about another person, not necessarily the audition for a lifelong partner. This perspective can relieve some of the pressure that first dates often carry, making the experience more enjoyable and less like a high-stakes interview. Encourage yourself to stay in the moment, appreciate the opportunity to connect with someone new, and remember that not every date needs to lead to a second one. It's about the experience, the conversation, and maybe the start of something new. So, temper expectations with a dose of reality and optimism.

Lastly, let's talk about post-date etiquette. Whether you felt sparks or not, communicating after the date can set the tone for future interactions with this person or how you handle dating moving forward. If you're interested, a simple message expressing enjoyment of the time spent together and interest in meeting up again can be a gentle yet straightforward way of indicating your intentions. If you don't feel a connection, it's okay to express that respectfully. Honesty, delivered with kindness, is crucial. It respects both your and the other person's time and feelings. Think of it as leaving a review after a pleasant experience at a restaurant—not mandatory, but certainly appreciated and helpful.

Navigating the first date in today's dating world involves balancing honesty with tact, enthusiasm with realism, and politeness with genuine expression. Planning thoughtfully, communicating, managing your expectations, and handling the aftermath with courtesy set the stage for potential future romance and personal growth in connecting with others. Whether the date leads to a long-term relationship or just a nice evening, each experience helps you understand yourself and others better in the world of relationships.

When to Disclose Past Marital Situations

Imagine you're setting up your favorite board game to play with someone new. You know the rules like the back of your hand because you've played it many times. But here's the twist — your new gaming buddy isn't just anyone; they might be your next close friend. Now, when do you explain that one quirky rule that always trips everyone up? Too soon, and you risk scaring them off; too late, and you might catch them off guard. Just like timing in games can be crucial, so is the timing when you choose to disclose details about your past marital situation in a new relationship.

The best time to bring up your past marriage is when the relationship moves from casual dating to something more serious — when trust is forming and you're both genuinely interested in building something deeper. It's about finding that sweet spot where you feel the relationship has potential and you're both comfortable sharing more personal aspects of your lives. This isn't about unloading baggage; it's about letting someone see the complete picture of what shapes you. It's like deciding when to share a secret ingredient in a recipe; you want to ensure they first appreciate the main dish.

Now, how do you go about disclosing? It's about weaving it into your conversations with care, not as a confession but as part of your life narrative. Focus on what this chapter of your life taught you. It could be about how it shaped your understanding of love or changed your perspective on what you seek in a relationship. Frame it positively, focusing on growth and learning rather than dwelling on the breakup details or your challenges. This approach shows that you're open and honest but also mindful of how your past experiences contribute to who you are today.

Anticipating reactions is also key. Reactions can vary widely, from curiosity and empathy to shock or discomfort, depending on their past experiences and perspectives on relationships. Prepare to calmly address their questions or concerns and reassure them of your current intentions and feelings. Their reaction also gives you insights into their empathy and openness and how they handle sensitive or unexpected information. It's like watching someone hold a plot twist in a movie — you learn a lot about them by observing their reactions.

Lastly, the importance of transparency must be addressed. Being open about your past relationship is crucial in building trust. It shows that you value honesty and are serious about building a relationship based on mutual respect and understanding. However, be mindful of maintaining a balance; respect your ex-partner's privacy and boundaries. Share what is necessary to communicate your experiences and the lessons you've learned without divulging details that might be too personal or irrelevant to your current path. This transparency is about being open and setting a foundation for a relationship that values honesty and open communication, creating a trusting environment where both of you can feel secure to share your lives and grow together.

Building Trust and Honesty in New Relationships

Imagine you're setting up a new gadget at home. You've got the instructions laid out, and you're ready to get it working perfectly. That's a bit like starting a new relationship—there's excitement, nervousness, and a hope that everything will run smoothly. The key component here, the one that makes all the difference, isn't just the shiny features; it's trust. Building trust from the outset of a relationship is like setting up a strong WiFi signal—it keeps the connection clear and strong, even when you're in different rooms or on different schedules.

Trust is built through actions and words that are consistent and reliable. It's showing up when you say you will, calling when you promised you'd call, and being honest about your feelings and intentions. Think of it as setting up a series of small, successful experiences that build confidence in one another. It's the small things that count here. If you've planned to meet at a cafe at three, be there at three. These acts of reliability create a secure foundation, just as a series of successfully executed tasks builds trust in your gadget's reliability.

Honesty about your needs and boundaries is equally crucial. From the get-go, it's important to be clear about what you need from a relationship and your limits. This isn't about laying down rules for someone else to follow but rather about opening up a map and showing them the terrain of your heart. What do you value? What hurts you? Being upfront about these things sets a clear course for the relationship and prevents misunderstandings that can lead to hurt feelings later on. It's like programming your preferences into a new app; it ensures that the output—your interactions and the relationship's trajectory—is more to your liking and suitable for your needs.

Dealing with baggage is something most of us bring to new relationships, whether we like it or not. Think of it as the apps and data you've transferred from an old device to a new one. Some of these are useful, like cherished memories and learning experiences, while others, like past hurts or insecurities, might need sorting through or deleting. The trick is not to let this old data overload or disrupt the new system. Share these past experiences with your partner at a pace that feels comfortable and in ways that add depth and understanding to your relationship. Let them know why certain things make you anxious or some days are more complex. This sharing can turn potential stumbling blocks into stepping stones, deepening your connection.

Continuous communication is like the regular updates apps get to keep them running smoothly. It involves regularly checking in with each other, not just about your day but about your feelings toward the relationship and each other. Are your needs being met? Has something been bothering you? These regular check-ins can help adjust expectations and address issues before they become problems, ensuring that the relationship continues to grow and adapt over time. It's about always keeping the lines open so neither of you feels like you're operating in the dark.

As you build trust and honesty in your new relationship, remember this is a process. Just like getting to know a new device, learning and adjusting to each other takes time. Be patient, keep communicating, and gradually, you'll find that you've built a secure and rewarding connection.

Moving Forward

In wrapping up this chapter, we've navigated the delicate beginnings of entering new relationships after significant life changes. From embracing your identity to finding safe venues, understanding the dating dynamics, and setting realistic expectations online, each step is geared toward fostering genuine connections. As you continue this adventure, remember the importance of building trust through honesty and open communication, ensuring that each new relationship has the potential to flourish. Now, let's turn the page and explore what maintaining these relationships looks like in the long run, ensuring they survive and thrive in life's everyday reality.

EIGHT

Resources and Moving Forward

Imagine standing in the middle of a vast library, each book offering a portal into different human experiences and knowledge facets. That's what this chapter aims to be for you—a library at your fingertips, carefully curated to guide, educate, and inspire you as you navigate the intricacies of a mixed-orientation marriage. Whether you're looking for legal advice, personal stories of resilience, or films that mirror your experiences, consider this your personalized reading nook, filled with resources to enlighten and support your journey.

Essential Reading and Viewing: A Curated List

Curated Books and Articles

Let's start by filling our virtual shelves with books and articles, like having coffee with experts and peers who've been through similar experiences. Imagine a book that feels like it's written just for you, with pages filled with words that resonate with your deepest thoughts and challenges. Here are a few to place on your must-read list:

- ***The Other Side of the Closet*** by Amity Pierce Buxton, Ph.D., unravels the personal and relational impacts of coming out in a marriage. Think of it as a guide through the emotional maze of mixed-orientation relationships, offering both the map and the compass to navigate this challenging terrain.
- ***Married to a Man, In Love with a Woman*** by Joanne Fleisher explores women's narratives in mixed-orientation marriages. It's like sitting down with a close friend who shares your unspoken thoughts and fears, offering camaraderie and understanding.
- For scholarly readers, articles from the ***Journal of Bisexuality*** or ***Journal of GLBT Family Studies*** offer academic insights into the dynamics in mixed-orientation marriages, providing a more analytical view that complements personal stories.

Recommended Documentaries and Films

Switching mediums, let's dim the lights and queue up documentaries and films that reflect the spectrum of experiences in mixed-orientation marriages. These visual narratives can be powerful mirrors and windows, offering insights and resonances:

- ***Out in the Open*** is a documentary that explores how various individuals and families deal with the challenges of LGBTQ+ disclosure. It's like a heart-to-heart conversation but in HD.
- ***The Case Against 8*** is a behind-the-scenes look at the legal battle to overturn California's ban on same-sex marriage. It offers legal insights and personal victories, a cocktail of

inspiration for anyone navigating marriage equality challenges.

Educational Materials for Families

For those with little ones running around, or perhaps just a family-friendly approach to discussion, incorporating educational materials can help open up conversations about diversity and acceptance:

- Books like *And Tango Makes Three* by Justin Richardson and Peter Parnell, which charmingly tell the true story of a same-sex penguin couple raising a chick, can be a gentle introduction to topics of love and diversity for children.
- Films like *Incredibles 2*, where themes of family support and teamwork can parallel discussions about the strengths of diverse family dynamics, turn movie night into a fun and subtle learning experience.

Updates and Reviews

Lastly, staying updated is like keeping your GPS on during a road trip; it helps you keep up with the ever-changing LGBTQ+ rights and stories. Regularly visiting websites such as *GLAAD* or *Human Rights Campaign* can provide you with the latest news, reviews, and discussions. Think of it as your daily newsfeed, curated to keep you informed and engaged with content that matters to your life and relationships.

As you bookmark pages, highlight passages, and reflect on the stories and studies shared, remember that each resource is a stepping stone on your path. They're here to offer you knowledge, comfort, and a reminder that no matter the complexity of your journey, you're not walking it alone. So, pull up a chair, pour yourself a cup of tea, and immerse yourself in the rich array of resources that await in your very own literary sanctuary.

Professional Services and Support Networks

Navigating a mixed-orientation marriage isn't just about emotional adjustments; it often involves untangling a web of legal, financial, and healthcare threads you didn't even know existed. Think of it as trying to assemble a massive, multi-level piece of furniture without the manual. That's where professional services and support networks come into play, offering you the right tools and instructions not just to assemble but to ensure your construct is sturdy and functional.

Therapists and Counselors

Let's talk about therapists and counselors, the unsung heroes in your support network. Finding a therapist who isn't just LGBTQ+ friendly but also experienced with mixed-orientation marriages can be like finding a coach who knows exactly how to tailor your training to your quirks. These professionals can provide invaluable guidance, offering strategies to manage your unique challenges. They can help you deal with complex emotions, improve communication, and support personal and mutual growth in your relationship. If you're looking for someone to add to your team, check out resources like the American Association for Marriage and Family Therapy, which offers a directory of therapists with diverse specializations, ensuring you find someone who truly understands the unique dynamics of your relationship.

Financial Advisors and Legal Professionals

Next up are financial advisors and legal professionals. Think of them as your navigators through the often-bewildering world of financial planning and legalities. Whether you're contemplating the implications of joint property ownership, setting up wills, or navigating the dissolution of a marriage, these experts can provide clarity and peace of mind. They understand that your relationship's financial and legal aspects aren't just about spreadsheets and documents; they're about securing your future and protecting your rights. Organizations like the National LGBT Bar Association can be a fantastic starting point to find legal professionals who specialize in LGBTQ+ issues and are sensitive to the nuances of your situation.

Healthcare Providers

When it comes to healthcare, the importance of finding providers who are not just inclusive but also explicitly supportive of LGBTQ+ individuals cannot be overstated. Knowing that you can speak openly about your life and receive care without judgment is crucial, whether it's a general practitioner, a mental health specialist, or any other healthcare provider. It's like having a doctor who treats your symptoms and understands your life's stressors and how they might affect your health. The Gay and Lesbian Medical Association (GLMA) provides a directory of healthcare providers committed to ensuring LGBTQ+ individuals receive competent and understanding care.

Relocation Services

Lastly, relocation services specializing in finding LGBTQ+ friendly areas can be a game-changer for those considering a change in scenery due to social or familial pressures. It's not just about moving to a new home; it's about finding a community where you can thrive, be yourself, and feel supported. Companies like Suburban Relocation Systems or even local LGBTQ+ advocacy groups often have resources or partnerships to help you find neighborhoods accepting and celebratory of your identity.

Navigating the complexities of a mixed-orientation marriage without the right professional support can feel overwhelming, like trying to decode a foreign language without a translator. But with the right therapists, legal advisors, financial experts, and supportive healthcare providers, you can build a network of professionals who understand your needs and champion your right to a fulfilling and authentic life. Whether it's ensuring your family is legally protected, managing your finances wisely, or maintaining your health, these professionals make the journey smoother and the load lighter. So, consider building your support team because, just like in any aspect of life, having the right support can make all the difference.

Workshops, Seminars, and Support Groups

Imagine walking into a room filled with people who understand your situation and share similar experiences and challenges. That's the essence of attending workshops and seminars on topics relevant to mixed-orientation marriages. These gatherings offer a treasure trove of insights where you can learn everything from communicating more effectively with your partner to understanding your legal rights and maintaining emotional health. Picture this: a workshop where you and other attendees dive into role-playing exercises that help you practice discussing sensitive topics with your partner or seminars where experts dissect the legal nuances of LGBTQ+ rights that directly impact your marriage. These events can be found in physical locations that foster community and solidarity and online platforms that offer convenience and accessibility.

Educational seminars are particularly invaluable. They serve as deep dives into specific aspects of LGBTQ+ issues, tailored to address the unique situations mixed-orientation couples face. Think of a seminar as a focused session where you can unpack the complexities of your relationship status, guided by experts who are there to provide clarity and actionable advice. Whether understanding how to navigate changes in your relationship dynamics or discussing strategies to handle societal pressures, these seminars equip you with knowledge that empowers you to make informed decisions and strengthen your relationship.

Support groups, on the other hand, are the backbone of emotional support for many couples in mixed-orientation marriages. These groups provide a platform to share experiences, challenges, and successes in a non-judgmental environment. Whether it's a local support group meeting in a community center or an online group that meets via video chat, your connections here can be lifelines. In these groups, you're likely to find support, friendship, and understanding from individuals who truly get what you're going through. The schedules for these meetings are often flexible, catering to their members' varied needs ensuring that anyone who needs support can find it at a time that works for them.

Specialized Programs for Children and Adolescents

Let's not forget the youngest members of the family. Workshops and seminars for children and adolescents from mixed-orientation families are crucial. These programs are designed to educate and support them in a way that's age-appropriate and engaging, helping them understand and embrace family diversity. These programs foster an environment of openness and acceptance through story-telling sessions introducing characters from diverse family backgrounds or group discussions, encouraging kids to express their feelings and ask questions. They help children make sense of their family dynamics and teach them the value of inclusivity and respect for all types of families. These programs often occur in community centers, schools, or even as part of local LGBTQ+ events, making them accessible to families looking for support.

Navigating a mixed-orientation marriage can be complex, but you don't have to do it alone. These resources are designed to guide, support, and empower you, from workshops that enhance your communication skills to seminars that deepen your understanding of legal rights and support groups that offer a shoulder to lean on. Specialized programs ensure that the kids grow up with a healthy understanding and appreciation of their unique family structure and are equipped to face the world with confidence and openness. So, take advantage of these opportunities to connect, learn, and grow alongside others who share similar paths. Whether walking into a seminar room or logging into an online workshop, you're stepping toward a stronger, more informed, and supportive family life.

Advocacy and Legal Support Organizations

Navigating the dynamics of a mixed-orientation marriage often feels like you're trying to assemble a jigsaw puzzle with pieces from different sets — challenging, sometimes confusing, but ultimately a rewarding process of creating a beautiful picture. In this endeavor, LGBTQ+ advocacy groups and legal support organizations are like the friends who pop over with the missing pieces and a fresh perspective that makes everything click. These organizations are not just support hubs; they're empowerment zones where you can arm yourself with knowledge, legal advice, and the comforting reassurance that you're not alone in this.

LGBTQ+ Advocacy Groups

Let's start with the backbone of support — the LGBTQ+ advocacy groups. These organizations are like your local neighborhood watch but on a grander scale. They're looking out for you and the LGBTQ+ community, ensuring safety, equality, and justice. National groups like GLAAD and the Human Rights Campaign (HRC) offer a wealth of resources, from educational materials to legal assistance, ensuring no question goes unanswered and no concern is unaddressed. They're the megaphones amplifying the voices of the LGBTQ+ community, including those in mixed-orientation marriages, in the halls of power, from city councils to the Supreme Court.

Internationally, organizations like Amnesty International and the International Lesbian, Gay, Bisexual, Trans and Intersex Association

(ILGA) provide a global perspective on the rights and challenges faced by LGBTQ+ individuals. They offer a bird's-eye view of global advancements and issues, connecting you with movements and changes beyond your local environment. This worldwide network can be particularly empowering, reminding you that the struggle for rights and recognition is a shared one, transcending borders and cultures.

Legal Support and Resources

Consider these organizations your legal eagles regarding the nuts and bolts of legal support. Lambda Legal, for instance, specializes in LGBTQ+ issues and has a robust track record of fighting for the rights of LGBTQ+ individuals in the courtroom, including those in mixed-orientation marriages. They guide everything from marriage and family law to discrimination and immigration. Their resources help you understand the legal system, ensuring you know your rights and how to protect them.

The ACLU offers direct assistance and advocacy for those dealing with specific challenges such as discrimination or parental rights. They're like the legal first responders, ready to step in when your rights are threatened, providing both legal representation and advice to ensure you're never left to fend for yourself in a legal storm.

Community Initiatives

Community initiatives add another layer of support, focusing on improving life on the ground for LGBTQ+ individuals and their families. These can range from local volunteer-led groups hosting community events to larger organizations driving policy changes at the city or state level. Engaging with these initiatives can be as rewarding as it is supportive. Volunteering, for instance, helps further the cause and connects you with a community of like-minded individuals who understand your situation and can offer personal insights and support.

These initiatives often work closely with local governments to ensure that LGBTQ+ individuals and mixed-orientation couples are considered in policy-making, from anti-discrimination laws to family rights. This grassroots involvement is crucial, as it ensures that mixed-orientation couples' specific needs and challenges are not overlooked but actively addressed, creating a more inclusive and supportive community environment.

Policy and Legislative Updates

Staying informed about policy and legislative changes is like keeping your GPS updated; it helps you navigate the ever-evolving legal system without getting lost. Advocacy groups often provide newsletters and updates on legislation that could impact your rights as part of a mixed-orientation marriage. These updates can be crucial in anticipating and reacting to changes affecting your family, from shifts in marriage laws to new protections against discrimination.

Engaging with policy advocacy also gives you a chance to influence these changes. Many organizations offer training on how to get involved in advocacy, providing you with the tools to speak out on issues that matter to you. Whether it's writing to your local representatives, participating in lobbying days, or simply spreading awareness in your community, your involvement can drive real change, ensuring that the laws and policies reflect the diversity and needs of all families.

In this rich ecosystem of support, every action, every bit of information, and every connection counts. Whether you're seeking personal support, looking to engage with community initiatives, or keeping an eye on legal aspects, these organizations offer you the resources to survive and thrive in your mixed-orientation marriage. So dive in, get involved, and remember you're always supported in this community, never alone.

Online Forums and Community Platforms

Navigating a mixed-orientation marriage can sometimes feel like trying to solve a Rubik's cube in the dark. You know there's a solution, but boy, could you use light! That's where online forums and community platforms come into play—they're like the flashlight you need, illuminating paths walked by others who've been right where you are. These spaces are not just about seeking advice; they're about finding your tribe, your support network, and sometimes, just a good old venting session with folks who get it.

Think of dedicated online forums as your go-to hub for everything from the "how-do-I-handle-this" questions to the "here's-a-hug" moments. Platforms like Straight Spouse Network offer a sanctuary for individuals in mixed-orientation relationships to share their experiences and resources in a supportive environment. Here, you can dive into discussions that range from coping strategies and emotional support to understanding the complexities of sexuality. It's like having a 24/7 support group at your fingertips, where you can anonymously share your deepest fears and highest hopes.

Social media groups also play a crucial role in creating communities that feel more like family gatherings than support meetings. Facebook groups such as Mixed Orientation Marriage Resources serve as bustling forums where members share everything from the latest articles on LGBTQ+ rights to personal stories of triumph and tribulation. These are where you can celebrate your small wins and find comfort during tough times, all within a community that cheers you on every step of the way.

Blogs and personal stories offer a more personal touch, providing narratives that might resonate closely with your experiences. Following blogs like Josh Weed's or reading through personal accounts on platforms like Medium can sometimes feel like reading pages from your diary. These stories offer a personal connection and practical advice woven through real-life experiences. They remind you that while every story is unique, the threads of fear, courage, love, and discovery are often shared.

Lastly, professional online networks can be invaluable, especially for those who face challenges in their professional lives due to their situations. LinkedIn groups or professional LGBTQ+ networks offer career advice and support from professionals who have navigated similar paths. They can guide everything from handling workplace discrimination to finding inclusive companies, making them an essential resource for anyone looking to balance their truths with their professional lives.

As you explore these online forums and platforms, remember that each post read, each story shared, and each connection made adds a piece to your puzzle. These communities offer more than just advice; they offer a mirror reflecting a multitude of experiences and a window into countless journeys, including your own. So, log on, reach out, and let the collective wisdom, warmth, and understanding light up your path.

Planning for the Future: Long-Term Strategies and Goals

Embarking on the path of a mixed-orientation marriage can sometimes feel like setting out on a vast, uncharted ocean. You have your compass, map, and a starry sky of dreams above you. But what about the tools and techniques to navigate these waters smoothly? That's where effective goal-setting comes into play, serving as your guide to help measure the distance to your aspirations.

Setting goals in a mixed-orientation relationship isn't just about jotting down desires and hopes. It's about crafting a blueprint that respects both partners' dreams across personal, relational, and professional spheres. Imagine sitting down with a cup of your favorite coffee and having a heart-to-heart with your partner about what each of you truly desires in the coming years. It's about aligning these visions and setting realistic, achievable goals, celebrating your needs and aspirations. Techniques like S.M.A.R.T. (Specific, Measurable, Achievable, Relevant, Time-bound) goals can transform these conversations into actionable plans. Whether planning for a dream vacation, buying a new home, or supporting each other through career changes, setting these goals together ensures you row in harmony toward your shared future.

Now, let's talk money—navigating financial waters can be daunting. Long-term financial planning is crucial, especially in mixed-orientation marriages where legal and societal uncertainties can impact financial security. Think of it as preparing for a long voyage; what supplies do you need to ensure you don't run into storms unprepared? This might include setting aside savings for retirement, planning college funds for your kids, or investing in properties that offer security and growth. Consulting with financial advisors who understand the unique challenges faced by LGBTQ+ families can provide tailored advice that ensures your financial plan is robust, flexible, and inclusive of all family members' needs.

But what about personal growth and education? The world is your oyster, and continual learning is the pearl you can cultivate individually and together. Whether picking up new skills through online courses, attending workshops that enhance your professional abilities, or even pursuing new academic degrees, education is a lifelong journey that keeps the mind sharp and the heart open. For couples, learning together or supporting each other's educational goals can strengthen your bond and keep the relationship dynamic and engaging. It's like updating your ship's equipment; the more up-to-date it is, the smoother your journey will be.

Lastly, consider the legacy you want to leave behind. This isn't just about assets or namesakes but about your impact on your community and the broader LGBTQ+ community. Engaging in advocacy, volunteering for causes you care about, or simply being open and honest about your relationship to foster greater acceptance and understanding creates a ripple of change. Your legacy could be love, resilience, and advocacy, guiding future generations in their mixed-orientation marriages.

As you chart your course through these strategies and goals, remember that the journey is as important as the destination. Every step together in planning your future prepares you for practical life and strengthens your bond and commitment to each other as you build your shared life.

Let these strategies guide you as you move into the next chapter. They'll help ensure that the journey you've embarked upon in your mixed-orientation marriage is as fulfilling and enriching as possible, filled with shared success, mutual growth, and enduring love that stands the test of time.

Conclusion

Well, we've reached the end of our journey together exploring mixed-orientation marriages. We've explored the twists and turns, the ups and downs, and everything in between, from understanding the very definition and dynamics of these unique relationships to navigating the emotional rollercoasters, unpacking the legal suitcases and setting up family picnics with all sorts of family dynamics. And let's not forget those courageous coming-out stories that perhaps left us all a bit teary-eyed but hopeful.

The heart of our journey, though, has been about fostering understanding, acceptance, and support. It's clear that these elements are not just nice-to-haves; they are essential for the well-being and flourishing of individuals in mixed-orientation marriages. The more society wraps its head and heart around these relationships, the more individuals feel validated and less isolated.

Remember, the vision of this book was not just to fill your heads with information but to empower your hearts to march confidently and lovingly in your unique paths. Our goal was to create a sense of understanding for the LGBTQ+ community and society, adding elements of acceptance and support.

I urge you to keep this book from gathering dust on your digital shelf. Use the resources we've compiled—a treasure trove in Chapter 8 awaits exploration. Reach out, connect, and remember, you're not navigating these waters alone. The communities, counselors, and legal eagles are all out there, ready to support you.

And the stories—oh, the stories! From Bailey and Jordan's dance of dialogue to Linda and Mark shielding their family with love and open communication. Let these real-life champions remind you that with resilience, understanding, and clear communication, fulfilling and robust relationships are not just possible; they thrive all around us.

Now, don't just sit there comfy in your reading nook. Get out there and advocate, share your story, join a support group, or lend an ear to someone who might need it. Every small action contributes to greater inclusion and understanding.

Remember, navigating a mixed-orientation marriage is a continuous journey of learning, growing, and loving in deeper ways. Keep an open mind, stay curious, and embrace the changes with a spirit of adventure. Human relationships constantly change, and staying informed and engaged is the best way to have a fulfilling experience.

As we close this chapter, I leave you with a message of hope and empowerment. With the right mix of support, understanding, and courage, individuals in mixed-orientation marriages can—and do— lead incredibly rich, rewarding lives. Here's to navigating the complexities of the heart with the map of knowledge and the compass of empathy. Here's to you, your partner, and a world that sees love in its beautiful spectrum.

Keep loving, keep fighting, and keep growing. Your unique story makes the world all the richer.

Now that you have everything you need to navigate and thrive in your mixed-orientation marriage, it's time to share your new-found knowledge and guide other readers to the same help.

Leaving your honest opinion of this book on Amazon will show other couples where they can find the information they need and support their journey in mixed-orientation marriages.

Thank you for your help. Knowledge and support thrive when we share our experiences—and you're helping me to do just that.

Scan the QR code to leave a review on Amazon.

Let's keep the love alive, passing on the torch of knowledge and support to others navigating mixed-orientation marriages. Your role in this journey is crucial, and I am profoundly grateful for your help in making these relationships stronger and more fulfilling for all.

Here's to continuing our journey together, armed with new knowledge and a shared purpose. Thank you for being an essential part of this adventure.

Warm regards,

Alex Harper

References

- *Stigma, Anxiety, and Depression Among Gay and Bisexual ...* https://pubmed.ncbi.nlm.nih.gov/31315511/
- *History of same-sex marriage in the United States - Wikipedia* https://en.wikipedia.org/wiki/History_of_same-sex_marriage_in_the_United_States
- *The Sexuality Spectrum* https://www.webmd.com/sex/what-is-sexuality-spectrum
- *Mixed Orientation Marriages: Factors Keeping ...* https://www.iamclinic.org/blog/mixed-orientation-marriages-finding-the-factors-that-keep-your-marriage-together/
- *Your LGBTQ Relationship: How to Talk About the Tough Subjects* https://www.thegaytherapycenter.com/gay-couples-counseling-how-to-talk-about-the-tough-subjects/
- *OurPath* https://ourpath.org/
- *Do Mixed-Orientation Marriages Always End in Divorce?* https://www.sflg.com/do-mixed-orientation-marriages-always-end-in-divorce
- *Mixed Orientation Marriage : Pathways to Success* https://mixedorientation.com/
- *How Affirmative Therapy Supports the LGBTQ+ Community* https://www.lyrahealth.com/blog/affirmative-therapy/
- *Move Past Gay Shame & Embrace Your LGBTQ Identity* https://mytherapynyc.com/gay-shame/
- *The Psychology of Shame: A Resilience Seminar for Medical ...* https://www.ncbi.nlm.nih.gov/pmc/articles/PMC7780736/
- *Marriage & Relationship Recognition Laws* https://www.lgbtmap.org/equality-maps/marriage_relationship_laws
- *Money and Marriage for LGBT+ Couples: What to Know* https://www.morganstanley.com/articles/lgbtq-financial-planning
- *Child Custody and Support Legal Issues for Same-Sex ...* https://www.justia.com/lgbtq/family-law-divorce/child-custody-support/
- *Estate Planning Considerations for LGBTQ Couples* https://www.nolo.com/legal-encyclopedia/six-key-estate-planning-issues-gay-lesbian-couples.html
- *Mixed Orientation Marriages: Factors Keeping ...* https://www.iamclinic.org/blog/mixed-orientation-marriages-finding-the-factors-that-keep-your-marriage-together/
- *Children with Lesbian, Gay, Bisexual and Transgender Parents* https://www.aacap.org/AACAP/Families_and_Youth/Facts_for_Families/FFF-

Guide/Children%20with%20Lesbian,%20Gay-Bisexual-and-Transgender-Parents-92.aspx

- *Mixed Orientation Marriages: Factors Keeping ...* https://www.iamclinic.org/blog/mixed-orientation-marriages-finding-the-factors-that-keep-your-marriage-together/
- *Resources for Mixed-Orientation Marriages* https://canyonwalkerconnections.com/library/resources/resources-for-mixed-orientation-marriages/
- *Mixed Orientation Marriage : Pathways to Success* https://mixedorientation.com/
- *Mixed Orientation Marriages: Factors Keeping ...* https://www.iamclinic.org/blog/mixed-orientation-marriages-finding-the-factors-that-keep-your-marriage-together/
- *Mixed Orientation Marriages: Factors Keeping ...* https://www.iamclinic.org/blog/mixed-orientation-marriages-finding-the-factors-that-keep-your-marriage-together/
- *Mixed Orientation Marriages* https://familydiplomacy.com/mixed-orientation-marriages/
- *Resources for Mixed-Orientation Marriages* https://canyonwalkerconnections.com/library/resources/resources-for-mixed-orientation-marriages/
- *What LGBTQAI+ Communities Should Know About Online Safety* https://staysafeonline.org/resources/lgbtq-communities-online-safety/
- *7 Ways to Get Your Self-Esteem Back After Divorce* https://www.psychologytoday.com/us/blog/constructive-wallowing/201608/7-ways-to-get-your-self-esteem-back-after-divorce
- *How to Improve Communication Skills in Your Relationship* https://jedfoundation.org/resource/how-to-improve-communication-skills-in-your-relationship/
- *Mixed Orientation Marriage : Pathways to Success* https://mixedorientation.com/
- *Marriage Equality: Global Comparisons* https://www.cfr.org/backgrounder/marriage-equality-global-comparisons
- *Financial Planning Checklist For LGBTQ Families* https://www.forbes.com/sites/jonathanshenkman/2023/03/13/financial-planning-checklist-for-lgbtq-families/
- *(PDF) Resilient Factors in Mixed Orientation Couples* https://www.researchgate.net/publication/247510576_Resilient_Factors_in_Mixed_Orientation_Couples_Current_State_of_the_Research

www.ingramcontent.com/pod-product-compliance
Lightning Source LLC
Chambersburg PA
CBHW072008150726

47999CB00002B/550